CONTENTS

CHARLIE CHAPLIN
THE ART OF COMEDY

David Robinson

THAMES AND HUDSON

Charles Chaplin's beginnings were far from auspicious. The man who, as the little tramp, was to become one of the most universally known and loved figures of the 20th century started his life in late 19th-century London in conditions of poverty and privation that recall the novels of Charles Dickens. Indeed, throughout his life, his favourite book remained Dickens' *Oliver Twist.*

CHAPTER 1

A CHILD OF THE MUSIC HALL

Chaplin's early years were spent in a poor district of London with 'pea-soup' fogs and gas-lit streets (right). Years later he was to take a nostalgic look at the milieu of his youth in *Limelight* (1952).

As the seventeen-year-old star of the music hall sketch *Casey's Court Circus* (opposite), Chaplin probably found the shabby streets of south London less romantic.

Charles Chaplin grew up in a humble area of London just south of the River Thames, comprising the parishes of Lambeth and Southwark. It was there that his parents Charles Chaplin and Hannah Hill met, and, in June 1885, married. At the time Charles Chaplin senior was twenty-two and Hannah not quite twenty. Evidently both young people were stage-struck: Charles already described himself as a 'professional singer', and, soon after their marriage, Hannah started to appear at the music halls under her stage name of Lily Harley. During this period the music hall was at the height of its popularity in Britain: the country boasted more than 270 variety theatres, 36 of them in London alone.

The son of a professional singer and actress

Charles Chaplin senior rapidly became a minor star of the music halls – popular enough to have his picture on the illustrated sheet music of the 1890s. Hannah's career clearly did not flourish; there are very few records of her professional appearances, and these were always in the most modest theatres and in the lowest position on the bill. Yet her famous son subsequently insisted that she had real talent for the stage and that it was she who had taught him the art of mimicry and his skill in observing and analysing physical behaviour.

When the Chaplins married, Hannah had a three-month-old son, Sydney, whose father forever remained a mystery. Charles later wrote in his autobiography, 'To gauge the morals of our family by commonplace standards would be as erroneous as putting a thermometer in boiling water'. The great Charles Chaplin was born on 16 April 1889, probably in Lambeth, though his birth and baptism are not recorded.

Chaplin's mother was the daughter of a poor bootmaker in south London. Despite her failed ambitions in the music halls, Chaplin regarded her as a gifted artist. He described how she would sit at the window of their lodgings, watching the passers-by and guessing their characters from the way they moved.

Chaplin's father was well enough known to be portrayed on the cover of the popular songs he performed. 'She Must Be Witty, She Must Be Pretty' was an ironic ditty about a man in search of a suitable wife. Prettiness and wit were not the only qualities he demanded: the song went on to explain that he also expected her to have a fortune of her own.

Programme.

This Programme is arranged under the direction of Mr. Geo. Adney Payne.

JUL 3— 1895

5.   MR. CHARLES CHAPLIN, Descriptive Vocalist.

Poorly clad and hungry

When Charles was one year old, his father went on a tour of American vaudeville theatres. Left alone in London, Hannah embarked on an affair with a more prominent music-hall star, Leo Dryden, by whom she had a third son, Wheeler. Not too surprisingly, when Charles Chaplin senior returned from his American tour and discovered this unforeseen addition to the family, he abandoned them.

Meanwhile, Hannah found herself abandoned in turn by Leo Dryden, who made a brief return merely to steal the six-month-old baby Wheeler away from her. She was not to see her youngest son again for almost thirty years. So Hannah was left to bring up her two remaining sons as best she could. Charles senior was ordered by the courts to contribute money to their support, but rarely did so; and Hannah earned what little she could by taking in sewing. The abandoned family grew poorer and poorer; the boys were ill-clad and mostly hungry as they moved from one wretched garret to another in search of somewhere cheaper to live. To add to Hannah's troubles, she watched her own mother, who lived nearby, become an alcoholic and being locked away as a lunatic.

The Poor Law School at Hanwell

In the summer of 1895, when Sydney was ten and Charles six, Hannah also began to show signs of mental

Chaplin's father (above) was to succumb, at the age of thirty-seven, to the endemic disease of the Victorian music halls – alcoholism. The managers of vaudeville theatres, who depended upon the sale of liquor for their profits, encouraged the artists to socialize with the patrons so that they would drink plentifully. Top: music-hall programme of a show in which Chaplin's father sang.

instability. When she was admitted to hospital, Charles
stayed with relatives and Sydney was sent to a children's
home. The family were reunited after a month or so, but
in the early summer of 1896 Hannah's condition
deteriorated again. This time the two brothers were
taken to the Poor Law School at Hanwell, on the
outskirts of London, an institution for children without
families. It was not an inhumane place – the children
were kept warm, clothed and fed; there was a swimming
pool, and some (though not all) of the children even
boasted toothbrushes. Yet the sensitive Charles clearly
felt acute emotional deprivation, particularly when
Sydney was rewarded for his good behaviour by being
transferred from the school to the training ship *Exmouth*,
a battleship used for training poor boys for sea service.
Sydney was later to turn his training – which included
gymnastics and music – to good effect.

After more than a year and a half in these institutions,
the two boys rejoined their mother and once more took
up their precarious existence together, trailing from
lodging to lodging. Within a few months Hannah had
another relapse and was committed to a mental hospital
while her sons were again placed in institutions. For a
few weeks at the end of 1898 they moved in with their
father and his new mistress. From all accounts the stay
was not agreeable: Charles Chaplin senior was often
drunk, and his mistress, who had a child of her own to
care for, resented having the burden of two more boys
thrust upon her. Everyone seems to have been relieved
when Hannah, in one of the periods of remission that
now became less and less frequent, was released from
hospital and took the boys to live with her yet again in
a back-street room.

Early music-hall experience

Young Charles' fortunes, however, soon took a sudden
dramatic turn. Still four months short of his tenth
birthday, he embarked on the career of professional
entertainer that would last for the rest of his life. Perhaps
during the short time they lived together, Charles senior
became aware of his younger son's gift for mimicry, and
persuaded a music-hall acquaintance, William Jackson,

Charles Chaplin
at seven years old:
an enlargement from
a group photograph
(opposite) taken when
he was an inmate of
the Central London
Poor Law School at
Hanwell. Despite its
name, it was situated in
the suburbs of London.

to give little Charlie a place in his troupe of child performers, the Eight Lancashire Lads. After six weeks learning to clog-dance, Charles seems to have made his first appearance with the troupe in *Babes in the Wood* at the Theatre Royal, Manchester, on Christmas Eve 1898. For the next two years he toured Britain with Jackson's Lancashire Lads.

The music halls themselves provided an incomparable apprenticeship in the crafts of the theatre. Every music-hall bill consisted of between twelve and twenty individual acts, competing fiercely for the approval of an impatient and demanding audience who could be hostile and unruly if it did not like what it was given.

Chaplin recalled with pride an occasion when the Lancashire Lads were playing animals in a production of

Although the buildings of the Hanwell School were old, its methods were humane by the standards of the 1890s. There was a swimming pool and extensive play areas; the dormitories were aired and heated, and the food was adequate. Yet, however enlightened its regime, this institution could not compensate a sensitive child like Chaplin for the loss of family affection.

Cinderella at the newly opened London Hippodrome. In the character of a cat, he introduced an improvised gag, cheekily raising his back leg, in a distinctly dog-like gesture, against the side of the stage proscenium. The audience loved it, though the management forbade him to repeat it, for fear of offending

the strict stage censorship of the times. Clearly, even at this stage, he saw his future in entertainment.

Odd jobs

Early in 1901 he left the Lancashire Lads: Hannah, once again out of hospital, apparently decided the life was not healthy for him. For the next two years Charles seems to have lived a hand-to-mouth existence on the streets of Lambeth and Southwark. In his autobiography he recalls some of the odd jobs he undertook in an effort to maintain himself and Hannah. He worked in turn for a barber, a shopkeeper, a doctor and as a page. He was briefly employed by a stationer, a glass-blower and a printer. Other enterprises included an attempt to sell old clothes in a market place, and a period that seemed to have made a particular impression upon him, when he helped some street vendors to make primitive toys from paper and cork.

Meanwhile, Sydney took advantage of his training on the *Exmouth* and (after falsifying his age as nineteen instead of sixteen) went to sea in 1901 as a steward and bugler on passenger boats plying between London and South Africa. Between voyages he would return to Lambeth and on these occasions the earnings he had saved would bring moments of long-remembered luxury into the lives of Charles and his mother.

His first part

In May 1903 Sydney returned home to find the fourteen-year-old Charles alone, having once more had to commit Hannah to a mental hospital. Sydney had by this time discovered his own talents as a performer, singing at ship's concerts to entertain the passengers. He announced his intention to stay in England and to find work in the music halls. Charles also came to the decision to seek a career as a professional actor. Presumably urged by Sydney, Charles walked boldly into a well-known theatrical agency, Blackmore's theatrical agency in the Strand, and announced he was an actor in search of employment. Either the confidence or the charm of this shabby little boy made an impression: Blackmore's sent him for an interview for the role of Billy the page in a touring production of *Sherlock Holmes*, the successful show co-authored by Arthur Conan Doyle and the American actor William C. Gillette. Chaplin was given the part; and the star of the forthcoming tour, H. A. Saintsbury, also engaged him to play a newsboy in his own play, *Jim: A Romance of Cockayne*, which was just about to go into production.

In *My Autobiography* (1964), Chaplin describes his early life: 'I had been newsvendor, printer, toy-maker, glass-blower, doctor's boy etc., but during these occupational digressions, like Sydney, I never lost sight of my ultimate aim to become an actor. So between jobs I would polish my shoes, brush my clothes, put on a clean collar and make periodical calls at Blackmore's theatrical agency in Bedford Street off the Strand. I did this until the state of my clothes forbade any further visits.' After a succession of odd jobs, including work in a shop similar to the one depicted at the top of the opposite page, Chaplin took the character of Billy the page in *Sherlock Holmes* in 1903 (opposite). The part was small but offered opportunities for physical comedy. In most of the towns where the play was performed, the local reviewers singled out the young Chaplin for praise.

In his youth Charles was very close to his brother, Sydney Chaplin (above, c. 1905). In later life he still relied on his elder brother's advice and management.

The play was a flop, but the debutant actor rated a favourable mention in the otherwise adverse press notices, for his 'most realistic picture of the cheeky, honest, loyal, self-reliant, philosophical street Arab who haunts the regions of Cockayne'. For more than two and a half years Chaplin toured the country in *Sherlock Holmes*, adding all the time to both his professional expertise and his human observation.

Evidently he earned a reputation for his comedy skills in the role of Billy. In October 1905 William C. Gillette, the creator of the role of Holmes,

do you really remember this? Plumers

Charlie Chaplin

presented a new one-act *Sherlock Holmes* comedy at the Duke of York's Theatre in London and followed it with a revival of the original play. Needing a boy to play Billy the page in both productions, he sent for Charles Chaplin. Thus, at sixteen years old, Chaplin became a West End actor.

Comedy sketches

In March 1906 the *Sherlock Holmes* tours finally came to an end, and Charles joined Sydney in a music-hall sketch, *Repairs*. Comedy sketches were a favourite feature of music-hall bills. Later the silent cinema would discover, in one- and two-reel slapstick comedies, a form remarkably similar to these ten-minute farcical playlets, full of acrobatic knockabout comedy. *Repairs* took the favourite comic situation of incompetent workmen attempting to decorate a house: Sydney played a painter and Charles the plumber's mate.

After ten weeks Charles left the company to join another popular and long-running sketch, *Casey's Court Circus*, which centred on the adventures of a number of boy urchins living in a slum courtyard. Chaplin, now seventeen, was one of the oldest in the company and the star of the show. He toured with *Casey's Court Circus* for

The programme for the Duke of York's Theatre, London, in November 1905 lists Charles Chaplin in the role of Billy and William C. Gillette (opposite) as Sherlock Holmes. In the spring of 1906, both Chaplin brothers joined the cast of Wal Pink's comedy sketch, *Repairs* (above). The seventeen-year-old Charles plays the plumber's mate (front, right); Sydney is the workman on top of the step-ladder at the rear of the scene. The piece was based on the well-worn comic theme of incompetent workmen who wreak havoc on the house they are supposed to repair – an idea Chaplin was to use, almost ten years later, in his film *Work* (1915).

more than a year. One of his most successful numbers was in a burlesque of Dick Turpin; and it was in this that he developed the comic run, with the characteristic way of sticking one leg out sideways and pivoting on the other as he turned corners, which was to become a trademark of his famous tramp character.

Fred Karno and the 'Fun Factory'

Meanwhile, Sydney had signed a contract with Fred Karno's Speechless Comedians on 9 July 1906. Karno was the greatest impresario of the music-hall sketch. He had begun his stage career as a gymnast, but established his name from the moment he presented his first comedy sketch in 1894. Within a decade he regularly had as many as ten sketch companies permanently on tour. The companies were managed and serviced from Karno's 'Fun Factory' in Camberwell, London. Here the costumes, properties and scenery, which was often very spectacular, were made, the scenarios written and the actors rehearsed until they performed their pantomime as perfect ensembles. Karno was a crude, uneducated and often unpleasant man, but he was evidently a genius at the creation of comedy. He had an extraordinary talent for inventing gags, for timing; and he had discovered that comedy could often be much more effective when offset with a touch of sentiment or pathos: this was a lesson that was to be of paramount importance to his most celebrated alumnus, Charlie Chaplin.

Born Frederick Westcott, Fred Karno (left) was an outstanding impresario of comedy in the English music halls in the years before the First World War. His sketches were short plays acted out in mime and energetic physical comedy, very like the first one-reel film comedies. Karno specialized in elaborate staging: in one sketch he represented a football stadium and in another an ocean liner.

Karno had several troupes on tour at the same time: they travelled in a variety of strange vehicles, including antique coaches, all prominently emblazoned with Karno's name (above).

A music-hall star by the age of nineteen

Sydney had joined Karno in July 1906, and by the beginning of 1908 was playing star roles and using his creative talents to write new sketches. He recommended his younger brother to Karno, who was not convinced, finding him 'a pale, puny, sullen-looking youngster. I must say that when I first saw him, I thought he looked much too shy to do any good in the theatre'.

Sydney persisted until Karno reluctantly agreed to give Charles a two-week trial. After seeing his first performances Karno hurried to sign him up for a two-year contract with a third year's option. Within a few weeks Charles was playing the leading roles in Karno companies. Two sketches made his name in the music

Stan Laurel, who also worked for Fred Karno's companies, described the Karno performance: 'No language was necessary because the acting of the [Karno] troupe was vivid and expressive.... All of the pieces we did ... were cruel and boisterous, filled with acrobatic humour and low, knockabout comedy.' John McCabe *Charlie Chaplin*, 1978

halls. In *Mumming Birds* the decor was a stage within a stage – a miniature music hall, with boxes at the sides in which comedians sat playing eccentric and obstreperous members of the audience, and reacting violently to a succession of terrible parody acts presented on the stage. Charles played a drunken man-about-town whose antics disrupted the entire show. His brilliantly observed characterization of an inebriate was so successful that it was written into several subsequent Karno sketches. Later it would also provide useful material for several early films. No doubt in his days around the pub-filled streets of Lambeth, and particularly in the period he spent with his own father, he had had the opportunity to observe at close quarters the symptoms of drunkenness.

In 1910 Karno offered Charles the leading role in a new sketch, *Jimmy the Fearless, or the Boy 'Ero*. At first he turned it down, but when he saw how effectively it was played by another rising young star of the Karno companies, he eagerly took it over. The actor from whom he took the role was Stanley Jefferson, later to become Stan Laurel of Laurel and Hardy. Charles was to remain almost six years with Karno, all the time studying and refining his comic art.

First love

When Charles was nineteen, he fell in love. The object of his affections was the fifteen-year-old Hetty Kelly, a dancer with a troupe called 'Bert Coutt's Yankee Doodle Girls'. Their acquaintance was brief, quickly brought to an end by Hetty's mother, either because she felt her daughter was too young for romance, or because she had greater ambitions for her than a liaison with a youthful music-hall comedian. Yet Charles never forgot his first love. More than fifty years later, in his autobiography, he wrote, 'Although I had met her but five times, and scarcely any of our meetings lasted longer than twenty minutes, that brief encounter affected me for a long

Between 1910 and 1913, as he toured the United States with the Fred Karno companies, Chaplin became famous for his performances as a comedy drunk in the sketches *A Night in a London Club* and *A Night in an English Music Hall*. The posters in the picture below, taken in San Francisco in 1911, show that he was already a star in vaudeville even before he went into films.

ALF REEVES PRESENTS
KARNO'S
PANTOMIME CO. IN
'A NIGHT IN A LONDON CLUB'

time'. In several articles and books, he later recalled Hetty, and as a mature man his often troubled love life seemed to be a constant search to rediscover that adolescent girl, 'a slim gazelle, with a shapely oval face, a bewitching full mouth, and beautiful teeth'.

Touring America

He was distracted from the pangs of love by a new adventure. In the autumn of 1910 he was chosen to star in a Karno company sent to tour the United States for twenty-one months. He was inspired by this great new world that 'throbbed with the dynamism of the future.... Space is good for the soul. It is broadening'.

After America, England seemed drab and disappointing. In his brother's absence Sydney had married and given up the apartment they had shared and which Charles had regarded as his first true home. After five months in England Charles was only too happy to embark on a second American tour in October 1912. He was appearing in Philadelphia in the summer of 1913 when he received the offer of a contract from the recently formed Keystone Film Company of Los Angeles. Charles Chaplin's film career had begun.

In September 1910, Chaplin sailed to the United States for the first time with a Karno company on the liner *Cairnrona*. Here he poses (centre) with two other Karno comedians, Mickey Palmer (left) and Mike Asher (right).

Someone – perhaps the presiding genius of Keystone, Mack Sennett – had spotted Chaplin in the course of one of the Karno tours and decided that he was likely material for film comedy. There is no evidence that Chaplin himself had ever given any thought to the cinema before this. He was, however, irresistibly attracted to the idea of doubling his Karno salary to a princely $150 a week.

CHAPTER 2

CREATING A CHARACTER

In his second film, *Kid Auto Races at Venice* (1914), Chaplin adopted the character of the tramp, which was quickly to make him famous throughout the world. The foolish little moustache (opposite) miraculously transformed him from a handsome young man to the absurd little tramp.

After failing to achieve success as an actor in burlesque and musical comedy, the Irish-Canadian Mack Sennett went to work for the Biograph film company in 1908. Studying the methods of Biograph's star director, the soon-to-be-great D. W. Griffith, Sennett graduated to become a scenarist and director in his own right – specializing in comedy, which was not Griffith's own forte. When the New York Motion Picture Company decided to set up a comedy studio in California in the late summer of 1912, Sennett was taken on as its production chief.

Mack Sennett, the head of the Keystone studios

Sennett had brought his principal stars – Ford Sterling, Fred Mace and Mabel Normand – from Biograph, and added new recruits from circus, vaudeville and,

As an impresario, Mack Sennett (below in his studio at Edendale in California) had many of the characteristics of Fred Karno. He was tough, uneducated and intelligent, with a highly developed instinct for creating physical comedy. Sennett had a long and turbulent love affair with the beautiful young comic star of the Keystone studios, Mabel Normand, who was twelve years younger than him.

if a suitably comic personage presented himself,
the streets. By the time Chaplin joined the company
in 1913, Keystone boasted the wildest imaginable
collection of grotesques – fat and thin, tall and short,
the men generally bizarrely whiskered and bowler-hatted,
the women in long skirts and dramatically feathered hats.
Keystone's comic world was firmly rooted in the familiar
realities of early-century, working-class America – broad
dusty streets lined with clapboard houses, grocery and
hardware shops, saloons, cheap hotels, dentists' surgeries,
bedrooms and kitchens, pretty women and stray dogs,
horse-drawn buggies and angular
automobiles erupting in smoke
and dust.

Chaplin (second
from left) with
(from left to right) the
three leading Hollywood
producers of 1914
– Thomas Harper Ince,
Mack Sennett and
D. W. Griffith – who
respectively directed
the three Hollywood
units of the New York
Motion Picture
Company – Bison,
Keystone and Reliance.

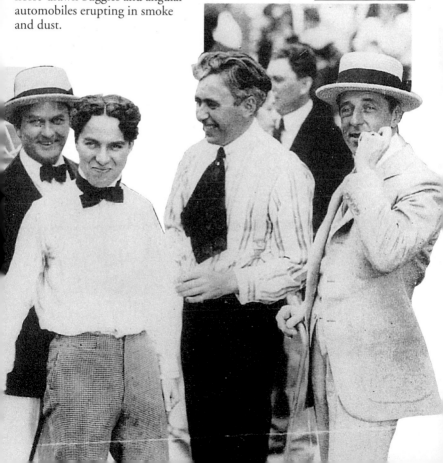

Chaplin arrives at the Keystone Studios for a day's work.

Speed is of the essence at Keystone

Chaplin arrived at the Keystone studios at the end of 1913. Accustomed to the meticulous preparation and rehearsal of the Karno sketches, he was shocked by the speed and reckless improvisation that characterized production at Keystone, which was committed to turn out two new films every week.

Some productions were more ambitious than others. The most elaborate might take several days to shoot and were filmed in sets built on the studio lot, sometimes with additional scenes shot on nearby locations. The simplest, filmed in a day or less, were the 'park' films, improvisations constructed around the ready-made facilities of Westlake Park – bushes, benches and the lake, which was always handy for a ducking when comic invention ran dry. Another favourite Keystone strategy was to send a film unit to any public event – a sports meeting or a procession – and to use the ready-made spectacle as an exciting background for impromptu foolery.

Chaplin's first film at Keystone, *Making a Living* (1914), was one of the more elaborate variety, with a simple story that casts him as a penniless and somewhat fraudulent dude with ambitions to be a newspaper

When Chaplin first arrived at the Keystone studios, he was horrified by the speed of work and the crudity of Keystone comedy. For his part, Mack Sennett was unsure about the subtlety Chaplin wanted to introduce into his films.

reporter. He wears a silk hat, frock coat, cravat, monocle and the drooping moustache of the traditional stage villain. There is nothing of the later tramp figure.

A cane and a small moustache: the tramp is born

Chaplin had a low opinion of the abilities of the director, Viennese-born Henry Lehrman, whom Sennett had brought from Biograph. He felt that all subtlety was sacrificed to breakneck speed; and that much of his best work was cut out in the editing. Moreover, both he and Sennett recognized that a new character was needed.

So it was that one day in the first week of January 1914 he went into the shed that served as the costume store on the Keystone lot to select a costume. When he emerged, he had created the tramp figure that remains to this day the world's best-known fictional representation of a human being. In his autobiography Chaplin said that he had chosen the costume so that everything should be a contradiction – the pants too big and baggy, the coat too tight, the hat too small and the boots too large. He added the swagger cane and the small moustache. 'I had no idea of the character. But the moment I was dressed, the clothes and the make-up made me feel the person he was. I began to know him, and by the time I walked on to the stage he was fully born.'

With his new tramp character, Chaplin introduced into his early films a richness of character and a range of emotion that was completely unprecedented in the crude knockabout comedy of Hollywood's early years.

The first film in which Chaplin used the costume and character was *Mabel's Strange Predicament* (1914), in which he plays an inebriated person who causes havoc first in the lobby and then in the bedrooms of a not very elegant hotel. The tramp character was first seen on screen by the public, however, in another film, *Kid Auto Races at Venice*. A typical Keystone 'event' film, shot on the Saturday afternoon of the week in which *Mabel's Strange Predicament* was filmed, *Kid Auto Races* was swiftly edited and shipped at once to the exhibitors. The film consists of only about a dozen shots and a single joke – the tramp's constant disruptions of the efforts of a film cameraman (played by Henry Lehrman) to film the races between boys in soap-box carts. Yet the essential appearance, gestures and movements of the tramp figure, and even something of his eventual character are already roughly, but firmly, sketched. During the next eleven months, the character was to develop rapidly, in the course of the next thirty-two Keystone films featuring Chaplin.

On the other side of the camera

Within weeks of his first appearance, the public had taken him to their hearts, and orders for the Chaplin films boomed. Chaplin, however, was increasingly

Mabel Normand was a gifted comedienne. While still a teenager, she worked as a model for some of the best New York magazine illustrators of the day. In 1910 she began to act in films for the Vitagraph Company. Moving to Biograph, she met Mack Sennett, who took her with him as his leading comedienne when he moved to California to establish the Keystone studios in 1912. When Chaplin arrived at Keystone, relations between the two stars were at first strained, particularly when Sennett allowed Normand to direct films in which Chaplin featured. She appeared in some of the films directed by Chaplin, such as *Mabel's Married Life* and *Getting Acquainted* (1914).

discontented with the work of the Keystone directors, Henry Lehrman and George Nichols. Matters were not improved when Sennett assigned Keystone's charming and clever star Mabel Normand to direct Chaplin:

In *Tillie's Punctured Romance*, Chaplin took the role of a con man and Mabel Normand that of his girlfriend (left). They were nominally supporting players to the famous stage comedienne Marie Dressler, who took the part of a stupid peasant duped by the tramp. The film took three months to make, an unusually long length of time for the Keystone studios (below).

Normand was three years younger than Chaplin and, as he was very much aware, much less experienced in comedy. In the end Sennett allowed Chaplin to direct his own pictures. His first efforts, *Twenty Minutes of Love* and *Caught in the Rain* (both 1914) were already superior to the general run of Keystone films.

From June 1914 and for the rest of his life, Chaplin directed every film in which he appeared, with the single exception of *Tillie's Punctured Romance*, the world's first feature-length comedy, directed by Sennett and released with great éclat in November 1914.

Chaplin made phenomenal progress as a film maker during these months at Keystone. Some of the films show him quite deliberately investigating and practising the unfamiliar techniques and possibilities of film, like cutting, linking scenes and close-ups. More importantly, he put to use the stagecraft and sense of mise-en-scene that he had learned in his years with *Sherlock Holmes* and the Karno companies.

●We have no scenario – we get an idea then follow the natural sequence of events until it leads up to a chase, which is the essence of our comedy.●
Mack Sennett quoted in Charlie Chaplin
My Autobiography, 1964

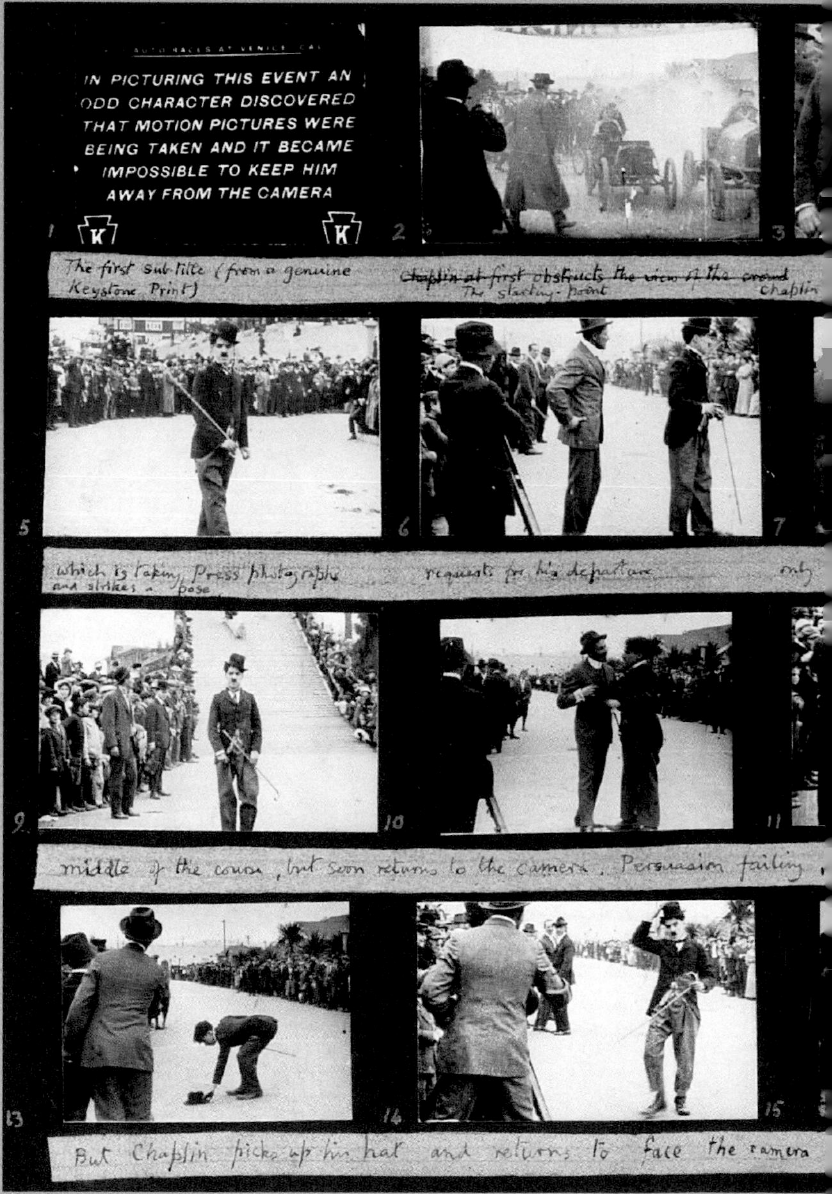

IN PICTURING THIS EVENT AN
ODD CHARACTER DISCOVERED
THAT MOTION PICTURES WERE
BEING TAKEN AND IT BECAME
IMPOSSIBLE TO KEEP HIM
AWAY FROM THE CAMERA

The first sub-title (from a genuine
Keystone Print)

Chaplin at first obstructs the view of the crowd
The starting-point   Chaplin

which is taking Press photographs
and strikes a pose

requests for his departure   only

middle of the course, but soon returns to the camera. Persuasion failing,

But Chaplin picks up his hat and returns to face the camera

s the view of the crowd   then gets in front of the camera

ifferent pose.   He goes off for a stroll in the

raman resorts to force.

r striking poses   and at shorter range

The first film in which Chaplin appeared in his famous costume of bowler hat, swagger cane and moustache was *Kid Auto Races at Venice*, directed by Henry Lehrman in February 1914 at the Keystone studios. The entire action consisted of the little tramp getting in the way of a cameraman trying to film the event. *Kid Auto Races at Venice* was filmed in just three-quarters of an hour. The last shot shows the tramp grimacing at the camera. Chaplin later recalled in *My Autobiography* (1964): 'The mechanics of directing were simple in those days. I had only to know my left from my right for entrances and exits. If one exited right from a scene, one came in left in the next scene; if one exited towards the camera, one entered with one's back to the camera in the next scene. These, of course, were primary rules. But with more experience I found that the placing of a camera was not only psychological but articulated a scene; in fact it was the basis of a cinematic style.' It was several months before he was allowed to stand on the other side of the camera to direct his first film, *Twenty Minutes of Love*, in April 1914.

He had acquired skills in visual story-telling, in pacing and inserting gags, whose sophistication was far in advance of the work of his Keystone colleagues. Films like *Caught in the Rain* and *Mabel's Married Life* (1914) combine narratives told with admirable clarity and minimal use of titles, with inventive and expert gag constructions. *The New Janitor* (1914) is built around a dramatic story that is the prototype for a notable later film *The Bank* (1915). In his final Keystone film, *His Prehistoric Past* (1914), Chaplin recalls the dream device of *Jimmy the Fearless*: the tramp falls asleep on a park bench and dreams that he is a cave man.

The Essanay Company

Chaplin's contract with Keystone ended in December 1914. Sennett and the directors of Keystone's parent company, the New York Motion Picture Company, were keenly aware of Chaplin's value, but would not meet his ambitious demand to be paid $1000 a week. The Essanay Company, however, with studios in Chicago and Niles, California, signed Chaplin at the unprecedented salary of $1250 a week, with a bonus of $10,000 on signing. Chaplin's relations with Essanay were never very comfortable. The studio's rather rigid, often penny-wise economies, were inimical to Chaplin's yearning for greater creative freedom and for time to develop and polish his films. His first Essanay film, *His New Job* (1915), set in a film studio (which was at least economical on sets) was shot in the company's Chicago studio. In February 1915 Chaplin returned to California, to make his next six films at Essanay's Niles studios or on location. After that he rented studio space – first the Bradbury Mansion, for *Work,* and finally the former Majestic Studios, both in Los Angeles – where he could work with greater autonomy.

At Essanay Chaplin began to build up his own little stock company of players, including Ben Turpin, a tiny man with severely crossed eyes, the heavy-weight Bud Jamieson, who was good at bullies and villains, and tiny,

Chaplin's first film with the Essanay Company was *His New Job*, in which he plays a would-be film actor. His co-star (above) was Ben Turpin, the first American film comedian who was known to the public by name.

dandified Leo White. More importantly, he discovered
Edna Purviance, who was working as a secretary when
Chaplin met and engaged her. She was to star with him
in more than thirty films and for several years also played
an important role in his emotional life.

The Tramp: laughter and tears

Although some of the fourteen films he made at Essanay,
like *In the Park* and *By the Sea* (both 1915), were slight
affairs, throwbacks to the old Keystone style of

Chaplin on set with
Edna Purviance
(above), who was chosen
by Chaplin to take the
leading female role in
his second Essanay film,
A Night Out (1915).

sation with the comedy offered by a particular location, others can be seen as significant steps in Chaplin's artistic development. *The Champion* (1915) contains a virtuoso sequence of pugilistic choreography that looks forward to the boxing sequence in *City Lights* (1931). In *The Tramp* the romantic and pathetic element that was to be the most distinctive characteristic of Chaplin's mature comedy is first fully manifested. Chaplin's

disappointment in love, when his hopes of winning the farmer's beautiful daughter (Edna Purviance) are dashed by the arrival of a handsome young fiancé, is poignant. The theme of the wretched tramp's romantic yearnings is developed with greater sophistication in *The Bank* (1915), where the tramp is the janitor and Edna the manager's secretary. The seeds can be traced to earlier work: the plot is a development of *The New Janitor* (1914); while he again explores the dream theme remembered from *Jimmy the Fearless*. Like *The Tramp*, *The Bank* ends with the tramp defeated; but for the fade-out he gives a little hitch-kick, shrugs his shoulders and walks off, away from us, into the distance and to new adventures as the camera closes in upon him. This kind of sad – or at least equivocal ending – was then something quite new in film comedy, and became something of a Chaplin trademark.

In *Work* another new element appears. The situation goes back to the old music-hall tradition and *Repairs*: the tramp

By 1915, Chaplin was famous. He appeared in comics (above) and in songs like 'The Charlie Chaplin Walk'.

Our Grand New Detective Serial: "THE GOLDEN FANG!" TURN TO PAGE 2.

Chaplin's films were adored by the soldiers of the First World War. One of the films he made for the Essanay Company was

Work (above), in which the tramp is the incompetent assistant of a house decorator, whose efforts to beautify a bourgeois home lead to its total destruction.

and his mate are totally incompetent workmen who cause havoc in the house they are meant to be decorating. This film stands out for its new and acute quality of social observation, in the relationship of the exploited tramp to his dictatorial boss; and the suspicions that separate the working men from their bourgeois employers.

Chaplin clearly intended to pursue these social concerns still further in a film to be called *Life*. Unfortunately, it was abandoned – perhaps it would have been too grim for audiences in 1915. A few sequences intended for the film were incorporated into the ironic *Police* (1916), in which the tramp, released from prison, finds the world outside harder than the one he has left behind. The fragments that survive from *Life* are set in a doss-house peopled by grotesques who bring to mind George Cruickshank's early 19th-century illustrations of London low-life as well as the novels of Chaplin's favourite author, Dickens.

The end of the contract with Essanay

Other Essanay films are memorable for other reasons. In *A Night in the Show* (1915) Chaplin adapted to the screen his old Karno warhorse, *Mumming Birds*, playing his original role of the drunken dandy who wrecks the show. In *A Woman* (1915) he gives an impersonation of a woman with great wit and subtlety: the machinations of the plot require that he disguises himself in this way in order to be near his girlfriend (Edna) after her parents have forbidden her to see him. In *Shanghaied* (1915) he demonstrates how a novel prop – a hired boat – could inspire a whole story and a whole new range of gags.

Chaplin's contract with Essanay ended in 1916 in acrimony and a costly lawsuit. His last film for the

company was a burlesque on the spectacular film of *Carmen*, just completed by Cecil B. DeMille and starring the great operatic diva Geraldine Farrar. To Chaplin's fury – he unsuccessfully brought a legal action – Essanay shot new material after his departure, in order to re-edit the film as *Charlie Chaplin's Burlesque on Carmen*.

The Mutual Film Corporation

These disagreeable incidents confirmed Chaplin's determination to seek working conditions that would guarantee him maximum independence in the future. He realized that he could now dictate his own terms.

In autumn 1917 Chaplin visited the site of his future studio, with members of his company (left). Sydney stands on the right of group; at the centre is Eric Campbell, the beetle-browed villain of the Mutual comedies, who was killed in a car crash on 20 December 1917.

After two years his films and his character were known in every country where there were cinemas. The outbreak of the war in Europe had done nothing to limit his fame and popularity: he was the idol of the fighting men of Britain and France.

I AM NOW WITH MUTUAL"

Below: on 26 February 19.. Chaplin (right) signed a contract with John R. Freuler of the Mutual Film Corporation guaranteeing him $10,000 a week and a bonus of $150,000.

CHARLES CHAPLIN & JOHN R. FREULER SIGNING CONTRACT

Sydney, who had now settled in America and taken over the management of Charles' affairs, negotiated a new contract with the Mutual Film Corporation. Chaplin's salary of $670,000 was the highest ever paid to any employee up to that time. He was given his own new studio, the Lone Star Studio, in the Colegrave district of Los Angeles, and there he built and consolidated his own regular company of collaborators. Edna, naturally, remained his leading female part and his constant off-screen companion. Of the newly recruited actors, the most important were Albert Austin, an old Karno trouper of dismal mien, and Eric Campbell, a giant Scot who, with his fiercely bristling eyebrows, was the finest villain Chaplin ever found, a true Goliath to his own David. A little later the company was joined by Henry Bergman, a fat and versatile character actor who worshipped Chaplin and remained for the next quarter of a century indispensable to Chaplin's working entourage. At Mutual Chaplin was joined by Roland (Rollie)

Henry Bergman (below) joined Chaplin in 1916 and remained at the studio as a character actor and general assistant.

Totheroh, a resourceful and patient photographer who had trained at Essanay and who photographed Chaplin's work to *Modern Times* (1936).

Revolutionary film-making techniques

Chaplin later described the eighteen months at Mutual from February 1916 to June 1917 as the happiest period of his life. In many ways it was the peak of his creative career. At twenty-seven years old, thanks to his apprenticeship in the music hall and theatre, he was confident in his command of the medium and also free to work in his own way.

For its times, his method of working was revolutionary. Up until then it was very rare for film makers to make two attempts at a shot. To take a scene over again could only be the outcome of some terrible technical catastrophe or an admission of a culpable error. Even the contemporary masterpieces of the great D. W. Griffith, *Birth of a Nation* (1915) and *Intolerance* (1916), were made with the expenditure of very little material beyond what was actually seen in the finished film. At Keystone, certainly, hardly a foot of 'waste' was tolerated.

From the moment he was his own master, however, Chaplin developed the habit of shooting a scene over and over again until he was perfectly satisfied with the

O*ne A.M.* (1916) was a daring demonstration of Chaplin's virtuosity (above) – a thirty-minute film in which he is essentially the solo performer. Chaplin plays a man-about-town who arrives home extremely drunk, and finds himself wrestling with all sorts of hazards as he attempts the perilous enterprise of climbing the stairs to go to bed.

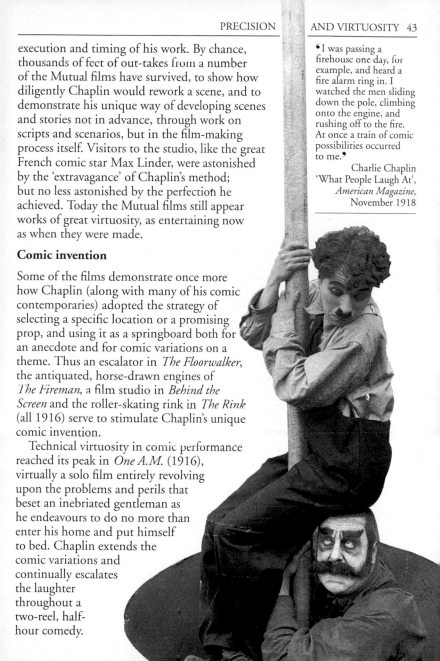

execution and timing of his work. By chance, thousands of feet of out-takes from a number of the Mutual films have survived, to show how diligently Chaplin would rework a scene, and to demonstrate his unique way of developing scenes and stories not in advance, through work on scripts and scenarios, but in the film-making process itself. Visitors to the studio, like the great French comic star Max Linder, were astonished by the 'extravagance' of Chaplin's method; but no less astonished by the perfection he achieved. Today the Mutual films still appear works of great virtuosity, as entertaining now as when they were made.

Comic invention

Some of the films demonstrate once more how Chaplin (along with many of his comic contemporaries) adopted the strategy of selecting a specific location or a promising prop, and using it as a springboard both for an anecdote and for comic variations on a theme. Thus an escalator in *The Floorwalker*, the antiquated, horse-drawn engines of *The Fireman*, a film studio in *Behind the Screen* and the roller-skating rink in *The Rink* (all 1916) serve to stimulate Chaplin's unique comic invention.

Technical virtuosity in comic performance reached its peak in *One A.M.* (1916), virtually a solo film entirely revolving upon the problems and perils that beset an inebriated gentleman as he endeavours to do no more than enter his home and put himself to bed. Chaplin extends the comic variations and continually escalates the laughter throughout a two-reel, half-hour comedy.

❛I was passing a firehouse one day, for example, and heard a fire alarm ring in. I watched the men sliding down the pole, climbing onto the engine, and rushing off to the fire. At once a train of comic possibilities occurred to me.❜

Charlie Chaplin
'What People Laugh At',
American Magazine,
November 1918

As Chaplin won more and more independence and control of his own productions, he broadened the range of emotions and sentiment that he intermingled with the comedy. In *The Vagabond* (1916) he plays a street musician who gallantly rescues a beautiful young woman (Edna Purviance) from the wicked gypsies who have kidnapped her. The tramp falls in love with her as they live a chaste idyll in their caravan in the woods; but a handsome young artist comes along, wins her heart and restores her to her rich family, leaving the little tramp heart-broken. The distributors clearly thought the end too sad, and Chaplin tacked on an improbable ending where the young woman and the artist turn back their car, and take him with them. Chaplin also considered finishing the film with the tramp throwing himself into the river, and being rescued by a woman so ugly that he instantly throws himself again into the water. Sentiment was always tempered with comedy: in this picture Chaplin is seen brusquely and practically washing and disinfecting the hair of the young woman he has just romantically rescued.

In these Mutual films Chaplin also carries to its greatest heights his special gift of comic transposition – the ability to make something appear, in the light of his comic vision, something else. Thus, for instance, in *Behind the Screen*, his back loaded with bentwood chairs, with their feet sticking into the air, Chaplin himself is metamorphosed into a porcupine. Comic transposition is brought to the peak of refinement in a scene in *The Pawnshop* (1916) when a customer hands the tramp, the pawnbroker's assistant, an alarm clock for appraisal. The clock becomes, in turn, a patient, a rare piece of porcelain, a safe, a can before, finally, being demolished. He hands it back to the astonished company with a shake of his head and a look of sorrowful sympathy.

The Rink offers opportunities for virtuoso comedy of a different, more physical kind, as Chaplin displays phenomenal skills as a roller skater.

The Vagabond is a comic melodrama in which he again develops a hopeless romantic liaison between the tramp and the heroine, played by Edna. *The Count* (1916), *The Rink* and *The Adventurer* (1917) are all based upon his favourite theme of social fraud – in the latter, he is an escaped convict masquerading as a guest at a party whose elegance he swiftly subverts. *The Adventurer* was his final film for Mutual.

In the films made for release by Mutual in 1917, Chaplin's stories became more complex and his gags more refined. *The Adventurer* begins with the tramp as an escaped convict, burrowing in the sand to escape the prison guards (with Frank J. Coleman, left). Having succeeded in throwing them off the scent, he dives into the sea to rescue Edna Purviance from drowning. Later, as a guest at an elegant party in her house, he gets into a variety of slapstick adventures before the prison guards arrive and set off in pursuit of him once more.

Cinema as art

By this time serious critics and commentators were beginning to discuss Chaplin's films in quite different terms from those applied to other comedies, and most other film production of the time. After *Easy Street*, *The Cure* and, above all, *The Immigrant* (all 1917), the word 'artist' was frequently used about this little clown working in the hitherto disdained medium of the cinema.

Significantly, these masterpieces were much longer in production than any Chaplin films before them. The first eight films under the Mutual contract were each made in four weeks; the last four films together took almost eleven months.

The Cure is a beautifully composed entertainment, set in a sanatorium whose patients are considerably revived when the stock of alcohol belonging to the tramp is inadvertently poured in to the mineral spring. The setting gave Chaplin a wonderful opportunity to surround himself with grotesque characters. His own adversary was, as usual in the films of the Mutual period, the ferocious giant Eric Campbell.

On 17 June 1917 Chaplin entered into a contract to produce his own films, for distribution by the newly formed First National Exhibitors' Circuit. Chaplin was meant to supply eight films in one year; but his working methods had now changed so much that it took four and a half years to make them. First National had no cause to be dissatisfied with the results.

CHAPTER 3

AN INDEPENDENT FILM MAKER

In the autumn of 1917 Chaplin began to build his studio in Los Angeles, on the corner of Sunset Boulevard and La Brea Avenue. Symbolically, he dug the first sod for the foundations (right) and inspected the unfinished stage (opposite).

Chaplin bought a plot on the corner of Sunset Boulevard and La Brea Avenue to build his new studio, which was completed in January 1918, and which served him for the rest of his film-making career in America. To reassure the local bourgeoisie, who had good reason to suspect the respectability of the film business, the exterior of the studio was camouflaged to appear like a row of cottages in an English village. The structures have survived to the present, and are today preserved as a historical monument.

Chaplin camouflages himself as a tree for *Shoulder Arms*.

The first film made there, *A Dog's Life* (1918), is a well-constructed comedy that draws metaphorical parallels between the daily existence of the little tramp and a stray mongrel dog who befriends him.

How to laugh at the war?

America had entered the war in 1917, and for his next film *Shoulder Arms* (1918), Chaplin audaciously set out to make a comedy set on the Western Front. His friends were nervous about the likely reaction to a film that dealt with the perils and privations of the battle front – the trenches, vermin, rain, homesickness, snipers, mud, floods and fear. As it turned out, Chaplin proved conclusively that comedy is richest when it is poised on the edge of tragedy. He metamorphosed the horrors of war into a cause of laughter; and his most appreciative audience was the men who had suffered them.

Now, however, for the first time since he had arrived in Hollywood, Chaplin's creativity seemed to fail him. No doubt the reason lay in troubles in his personal life. His relationship with Edna

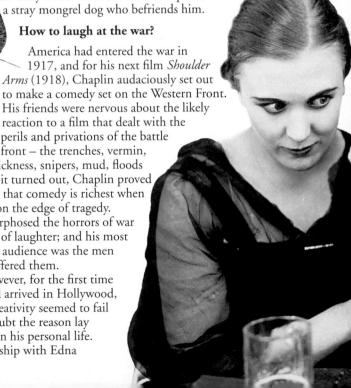

Purviance, who for five years had supplied support, companionship and love, had ended, though they continued to work together for several years. Early in 1918 he met a sixteen-year-old child actress, Mildred Harris, in whom perhaps he saw something of his first love, Hetty Kelly. In September he married her abruptly after being told (incorrectly as it happened) by her mother that she was pregnant. The marriage was doomed from the start: a naive seventeen-year-old girl could not provide suitable companionship for a man of Chaplin's creative energy. A child might have helped their relationship; but on 7 June 1919 Mildred

Chaplin was irritated by Hollywood imitators, who shamelessly copied his costume and comedy. He was more tolerant of Billie Ritchie (below and opposite), a former Karno comedian who claimed to have invented the tramp costume.

In *A Dog's Life* the tramp adopts a stray dog called Scraps. Chaplin draws parallels between the struggle for existence of man and animal. In the photograph on the left he is pictured with Edna Purviance, who starred in the film. Louis Delluc, who wrote the first serious study of Chaplin in the 1920s, thought it was 'the first complete work of art the cinema has. It is classical. It *exists*'.

The Kinematograph
and Lantern Weekly
N° 641 Vol 35   August 71919
6ᵈ

Sunnyside

gave birth to a severely handicapped son, who died three days later. The marriage dragged on wretchedly, to end in an unseemly divorce in November 1920.

Jackie Coogan, a star at four years old

Paradoxically, it was as if the trauma of his child's death somehow reactivated Chaplin. Before it he struggled painfully to complete a minor comedy with a rural setting, *Sunnyside* (1919), after which he had made a desultory start on a new film provisionally entitled *Charlie's Picnic*.

A mere ten days after his son's death, however, he had begun to audition children for the film, which was

At the time of filming *Sunnyside*, Chaplin was fascinated by Diaghilev's Ballets Russes and their star, Nijinski. This sequence (below) is a homage to Nijinski's legendary performance in *L'Après-midi d'un faune*. After being tossed by a bull, the unconscious tramp dreams he is awakened by four nymphs who lead him into an Arcadian dance.
Two years later, in 1921, *The Kid* (opposite right) was a great success. Negotiations with his distributors were not as cordial as this picture (opposite left) suggests.

eventually to become *The Kid* (1921). The inspiration seems to have come partly from his fascination with a four-year-old performer, Jackie Coogan, who appeared in his parents' vaudeville act. With Jackie as his co-star,

Chaplin worked out a story in which the tramp becomes surrogate father to a baby abandoned by his unmarried mother. While their relationship produces scenes of high comedy, the poignancy of the scenes in which the tramp fights to prevent the child being taken into public institutions is clearly inspired by bitter memories of his own childhood.

The shooting of *The Kid* was beset with problems. To fulfil his contract, Chaplin had to interrupt production to finish the film he had already begun, now renamed *A Day's Pleasure* (1919). Moreover, the Chaplin brothers had to spirit the negative to safety when Mildred's lawyers threatened to sequester it as security against an eventual divorce settlement. Finally, Chaplin had disputes with First National over the advance for the distribution rights. Nevertheless, the film proved a sensational success, making Jackie Coogan a world celebrity. For many, *The Kid* remains Chaplin's masterpiece.

'All children in some form or another have genius; the trick is to bring it out in them. With Jackie it was easy. There were a few basic rules to learn in pantomime and Jackie very soon mastered them. He could apply emotion to the action and action to the emotion, and could repeat it time and time again without losing the effect of spontaneity.'

Charlie Chaplin
My Autobiography, 1964

The pathos and comedy and the miraculous performance that Chaplin won from the four-year-old Jackie Coogan in *The Kid* have lost nothing with the years. Perhaps Chaplin saw in the child something of himself as an urchin struggling to survive on the streets of London in the 1890s. The precocious child goes into business with the little tramp (who is looking after the abandoned child) breaking windows, while his foster-father follows afterwards, offering his services as a glazier. This satisfactory arrangement is interrupted when the child becomes ill and Chaplin calls in an inquisitive doctor (played by Jules Hanft) who questions the true origins of the little boy.

A trip to Europe

With the completion of *The Kid* and the
settlement of his divorce, Chaplin's life seemed
to have become more calm. He finally
steeled himself to seeing his ailing mother
once more, and arranged for her to live in
Hollywood, though he seems to have found it
too painful to meet her very often. The last three
films due under his First National contract – *The
Idle Class* (1921), *Pay Day* (1922) and *The Pilgrim*
(1922) – were completed smoothly, though
(at least by former studio standards) slowly.

   Between *The Idle Class* and *Pay Day*
Chaplin took a holiday to visit Europe
for the first time since he had left
England with the Karno company
in 1912. He had changed and
so, after four years of war,
had Europe. In London
and Paris he was
lionized, mobbed by
the crowds and entertained
by the great men and women
of the day. In England he made

some nostalgic pilgrimages in search of the places associated with his youth; and he was shocked to learn that Hetty Kelly had died three years before, a victim of the influenza epidemic at the end of the war.

On his return to Los Angeles in October, Chaplin set about completing his final First National films. *Pay Day* unusually casts him as a working man and hen-pecked husband. In *The Pilgrim* he plays an escaped convict who is mistaken for the new minister of a small town. Chaplin's satire on religious bigotry was criticized by the more narrow-minded censors and church authorities.

The stars rebel

In 1919 Chaplin, his friends and fellow-stars Mary Pickford and Douglas Fairbanks, and America's leading director D. W. Griffith became convinced (even though their salaries were huge) that they and other stars were being exploited by the ever more monopolistic distribution system. On 5 February they drew up contracts to form the United Artists Film Corporation, a company to distribute their own films and those of other artists who wished to join them. 'The lunatics',

By the early 1920s Chaplin's fame had spread far and wide. In 1921 he visited Europe, where he was entertained by celebrities like H. G. Wells (opposite). A board game, 'Chase Me Charlie' (centre), based on the character of the tramp, was even devised. Below: a scene from *The Pilgrim* of the same period.

Left: on 17 April 1919 Douglas Fairbanks (left), Chaplin (centre), D. W. Griffith (right) and Mary Pickford (seated) formally created United Artists, a company to distribute their own films.

said one disgruntled distributor, 'are taking over the asylum.'

Having themselves contributed several films for United Artists distribution, the other partners were understandably impatient for Chaplin to complete his obligations to First National, since the success of the venture depended on a steady supply of product. As it happened, Chaplin's first United Artists film, *A Woman of Paris* (1923), was a disappointment in commercial terms, even though it was to be hailed as one of his greatest artistic achievements.

Chaplin had long wished to make a dramatic film. Moreover, he was eager to find a vehicle to launch Edna Purviance on an independent career. Since their 'emotional estrangement', as Chaplin called it, Edna had matured, had begun to drink, and had become less adept at comedy.

A melodrama rejected by the public

Chaplin derived the idea of *A Woman of Paris* from meetings with a notorious celebrity of the times, Peggy Hopkins Joyce, the original 'gold-digger', famous for marrying and profitably divorcing millionaires. Peggy's reminiscences, together with Chaplin's recent impressions of European high society, gave him the idea for a story about a country girl who comes to Paris and becomes the mistress of a rich man. Years later she meets her first love, from whom she was separated by chance, and who is now a struggling painter. Her attempt to renew the liaison only leads to tragedy.

The plot might have served any old stage or screen melodrama. What was new was the subtlety and sophistication of Chaplin's narrative style. The observation and visual sense that had formerly been exercised in creating slapstick gags was now used to give visual expression to the nuances of behaviour.

Adolphe Menjou and Edna Purviance (below) established a new, realistic acting style for films of social comedy through the sophistication of their performances in *A Woman of Paris*.

During a brief visit to Berlin in 1921, Chaplin met the tempestuous Polish-born film star Pola Negri (opposite). When she arrived in Hollywood in 1923, the acquaintance ripened into romance and an announcement of their forthcoming marriage – which did not however materialize. During their engagement, Pola took a great interest in the building of Chaplin's new house on Summit Drive (left). He jokingly called its architectural style 'California Gothic'. It remained his home until his departure from America in 1952.

A Woman of Paris was to have a lasting influence on social comedy in the American cinema, and Ernst Lubitsch, subsequently a master of the form, acknowledged his debt to Chaplin. Chaplin's four young assistants on the film, Edward Sutherland, Monta Bell, Jean de Limur and Henri d'Abbadie d'Arrast, were all to become gifted directors of comedy in their own right.

Few films have ever received such an enthusiastic and unanimous response from the press. Yet the public rejected the film. Perhaps the press notices themselves discouraged audiences, by assuring them that this was a work of art when the great public looked to Chaplin for laughter. Worse, their idol only appeared in the film for a brief moment, unbilled in the part of a comic porter on a railway station. Censorial disapproval in many states added to commercial failure. Hurt and disappointed, Chaplin refused for many years after the first release to permit the film to be seen at all. Only at the very end of his life did he add a musical track for a reissue – which proved little more successful than the first release.

The Gold Rush

Chaplin often said that *The Gold Rush* (1925) was the film by which he would most wish to be remembered. Again, he was to make comedy out of the least likely subjects. The idea for the film came to him when he saw some stereograms of the Klondike gold rush while visiting Pickfair, the home of Douglas Fairbanks and Mary Pickford. At about the same time he also read a book about the Donner party disaster. In 1846 George Donner had led a party of migrants on the trail to California: their privations in the snowbound Sierra

Douglas Fairbanks jokingly feigns boredom while visiting the Chaplin studio with his wife Mary Pickford in April 1919,

at the time of the formation of United Artists.

Nevada became so acute that some of the survivors resorted to eating the corpses of their comrades. Out of these grim themes Chaplin created one of his richest comedies.

The film was partly shot on location at Truckee, beside Lake Tahoe, high in the Sierra Nevada, and partly on vast sets simulating snowy wastes, built at the studio where the actors sweated in arctic furs under the Californian summer sun.

Chaplin's first choice for his female part was Lillita McMurray, who had already played a role in *The Kid*.

In *The Gold Rush*, the tramp is one of the thousands of hopefuls seeking their fortunes in the snowy wastes. He encounters a bear, a murderer and a friendly prospector who, in moments of hallucination, mistakes him for a plump chicken ready to slaughter and roast. He falls in love with a dance-hall girl – played by Georgia Hale (left in the poster) – who is finally conquered by his sincerity. The end shows the tramp, now rich from a gold strike, about to marry her. In this image (left), Chaplin allows the anguish of life in the frozen wastes to break through the comedy.

'It is paradoxical that tragedy stimulates the spirit of ridicule ... ridicule, I suppose, is an attitude of defiance. We must laugh in the face of our helplessness against the forces of nature – or go insane.'
Charlie Chaplin
My Autobiography, 1964

In *The Gold Rush*, starvation and hunger – of which Chaplin had had first-hand experience in childhood – become the theme for hilarious comedy. In one of the most famous scenes from the film, the tramp and his fellow-prospector are reduced to cooking and eating one of the tramp's disreputable boots. The tramp stews the boot with all the flair of a gourmet cook, before proudly serving it to his companion and himself. In this picture he savours the laces as if they were spaghetti. Subsequently he handles the sole as if it were some fine fish, extracting the nails like delicate bones. The boots used for the scene were made of liquorice; and it was reported that after three days of retakes, Chaplin and his fellow actor Mack Swain suffered inconvenient laxative effects from consuming so much of it.

Perhaps the most famous scene in all Chaplin's work was the dance of the bread rolls (left) from *The Gold Rush*. Two forks stuck into bread rolls became, in his deft hands, a pair of legs with comically booted feet, with which he performed a brilliant little dance routine. He did not invent the gag, but Chaplin's virtuosity made it unique. At the premiere at the Delphi Cinema, Berlin, the audience applauded the scene so much that the management rolled back the film and presented an encore. Similar incidents were reported from other cities. In London, the infant BBC broadcast a programme consisting only of ten minutes of laughter during an actual performance.

She was still not sixteen years old, though the studio publicity department described her as being nineteen and renamed her Lita Grey. After eight months, shooting was suddenly halted when she was discovered to be pregnant. Once more Chaplin found himself trapped in a shotgun marriage, doomed to failure and unhappiness.

The Gold Rush was resumed and completed with a new actress, the charming Georgia Hale, in the leading female role. Released in August 1925, the film proved to be one of Chaplin's greatest critical and commercial successes.

Chaplin's private life, however, was in crisis. Lita Grey had given birth to two sons – Charles Spencer in May 1925 and Sydney Earle in March 1926. Yet Chaplin evidently had little wish to return to the handsome Hollywood home on Summit Drive that he built only three years before. Following the premiere of *The Gold Rush*, he spent two months in New York, where he had a love affair with the dazzling young actress Louise Brooks.

I n 1942 Chaplin composed a new musical accompaniment for *The Gold Rush*. The original subtitles were replaced by a commentary, in which he names the tramp 'The Little Fellow'. He also altered the ending of the film, removing the embrace at the end (left).

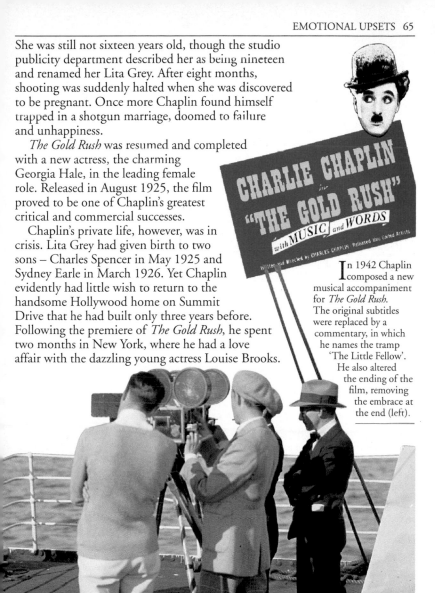

Monkey business: *The Circus*

Returning to Hollywood, Chaplin threw himself into work on his next film, *The Circus* (1928). In this case Chaplin first conceived the climax of the film and then built up the rest of the story around it. The climactic scene is an escalation of comic terror when, standing in for the high-wire star, the tramp finds himself on a rope high above the circus ring, without a net. His safety harness comes loose; he is attacked by monkeys who rip off his trousers. He has forgotten his tights.

In the story the tramp is cast as the usual vagrant. Chased into the circus ring by the police, he proves so funny that he is engaged as a clown. The only problem is that he is only funny when he does not intend to be. He falls in love with the daughter of the sadistic circus proprietor and defends her from her father; but his idyll is ended with the arrival of a new star, the high-wire walker whose place he so disastrously attempts to usurp. At the end the circus moves off, leaving him a solitary figure in the ring of trodden grass.

The high-wire star was played by Harry Crocker, a handsome, patrician young man from a rich San

The Circus also involved a scene in a lion's cage, for which Chaplin did over two hundred takes. One of the lions was far from docile; and Chaplin later said that the fear on his face in the finished scene was quite real.

Francisco banking family. Crocker became indispensable in the story and for the gag conferences that had become an essential part of the Chaplin method since Mutual days. Having roughly blocked out the action of his film, Chaplin would sit day after day, sketching out gags and action for the next 'faction' (the studio term for a sequence) to be filmed. A secretary would note down every good gag; only when Chaplin felt he had enough new ideas to inspire him would he begin to shoot. Once each sequence was finished, the process and the conferences would begin again.

A series of disasters: storms, fire and divorce

From the start *The Circus* was beset by misfortune. Production was first delayed when the circus tent specially constructed for the production was damaged by storms. A fault in the laboratory ruined all the material

Henry Bergman (below, with Chaplin) played the role of a clown in *The Circus*. Though Bergman's early career was on the operatic and musical stage, he claimed that it was he who taught Chaplin and his fellow actor Harry Crocker to walk the tightrope. Bergman's dog-like devotion to Chaplin, in the role of all-purpose assistant and character actor, often caused tension with other studio personnel, who regarded him as sycophantic. Bergman also ran a restaurant in Hollywood, called Henry's, which – thanks largely to Chaplin's regular patronage – became a well-known rendez-vous for stars of the 1920s. Bergman's final screen appearance was in *Modern Times*, as a civic official at the unveiling of a monumental statue.

shot in the first weeks. Nine months into production the studio was badly damaged by fire. The US government began to pursue Chaplin for alleged tax underpayment of more than a million dollars.

It was also the moment when Lita Grey, who was still only nineteen, chose to walk out of the family house with her two children. Encouraged by an uncle who was a lawyer, she filed extraordinary divorce proceedings against Chaplin himself, his studio, company, chauffeur, studio manager, the National Bank of Los Angeles and the Bank of Italy. The charges of cruelty were couched in lurid and humiliating detail. Receivers put the studio

The making of *The Circus* was a succession of nightmares for Chaplin. Not only had some film been ruined in the laboratory but a fire (left) had also destroyed the set on 28 September 1926. The divorce proceedings brought by Lita Grey (centre, taking the oath in court) only added to his problems. Nevertheless, Chaplin was defended by a group of French intellectuals, including René Clair: 'There is hardly anything we can say about Chaplin that has not already been said. And yet all that has been said is still insufficient. The public does not yet know that Chaplin is the greatest dramatic author, the greatest creator of fiction alive. His talent as an actor overshadows his genius as an author, and the majority of critics still see in him only a "mime of genius", a "sublime clown" – epithets that do not do him justice. Chaplin is more than that. He is, of course, an actor, and one of the best. But other great actors can on occasion be as good. Whereas as an author he is unique, and no other film author can be compared to him.'

René Clair
Reflections on the Cinema, translated by Vera Traill, 1953

under guard and opened up the safe and vaults – fortunately Chaplin had had the foresight to take the negative of *The Circus* to a safe place.

After months of sensational publicity, the divorce suit was eventually resolved. Lita Grey was awarded $600,000, while a $100,000 trust fund was set up for each of the couple's two sons; it was the largest settlement in American legal history up to that time.

It was a tribute to Chaplin's immense and worldwide popularity that his reputation survived this sordid case almost unscathed. When some women's clubs attempted to organize boycotts of Chaplin films, Chaplin found support from a group of French intellectuals, including Louis Aragon, René Clair, Germaine Dulac and Man Ray; he was even invited to emigrate to the USSR in order to escape the 'hypocrisy' of capitalism.

After eight months' enforced suspension of activities in his studio, Chaplin was finally able to resume work on *The Circus*. It was released in January 1928, and today remains wonderfully fresh and lively, betraying little of the troubles that plagued its production.

The arrival of the talkies

While Chaplin had been wrestling with *The Circus* and divorce, Hollywood had experienced a revolution: the talking picture had arrived. The first film with a synchronized musical accompaniment, *Don Juan* (directed by Alan Crosland) was premiered on 6 August 1926, the first all-talkie film, *Lights of New York* (directed by Bryan Foy), on 8 July 1928. One of the earliest films with a synchronized score was *The Better 'Ole*, which featured Sydney Chaplin, who had left his brother to make a brief career for himself as a comedy star.

The revolution shook the whole of Hollywood. For the studios it meant raising new capital for the enormous investment in sound equipment. Even the greatest stars found their careers at risk if their physical beauty was not matched (as it often was not) by their voices and diction: Georgia Hale was among those whose film careers ended abruptly. For Chaplin the problem was particularly acute. More than anyone else he had made the silent pantomime a universal language to command and

The first meeting of the tramp and the flower girl in *City Lights* flows, said the writer Alistair Cooke, 'as easily as water over pebbles'. Yet this simple-seeming scene by the girl's flower-stand gave Chaplin more trouble than almost any other he ever shot, taking weeks of work. More than forty years later he recalled, 'We took this day after day after day. She'd be doing something which wasn't right. Lines. A line. A contour hurts me if it's not right. She'd say, "Flower, sir?" I'd say, "Look at that! Nobody says, 'flower' like that." She was an amateur.'

captivate a worldwide audience. Could he risk allowing that audience to shrink to include only those who could understand English? Moreover, every spectator had his own fixed idea about the tramp. How could Chaplin now give him a voice, and what would that voice and accent be? Chaplin truculently told interviewers that he believed sound films had no future, and embarked on a new silent picture, which was to be *City Lights*.

The story of a woman who recovers her sight: *City Lights*

For more than a year – and even after shooting had begun – he worked on the story, inventing, refining, rejecting. From the very start, however, he had two clear ideas – about the story (which concerned a blind girl), and the final scene.

City Lights was an ideal silent picture, and nothing could deter me from making it. But I was up against several problems. Since the advent of talkies, which had now been established for three years, the actors had almost forgotten how to pantomime. All their timing had gone into talk and not action.*

Charlie Chaplin
My Autobiography, 1964

The finished story was admirable in the simplicity of its structure. Wandering the great, unfriendly city, the tramp befriends a fellow waif, a poor blind flower girl. One day he learns that the girl's sight may be restored if she goes to Vienna for an operation and sets about raising the necessary money, working as street cleaner and prize fighter to do so. He meets an alcoholic millionaire, whom he has once saved from suicide. Drunk and in expansive mood, the millionaire gives him the money, which the tramp in turn gives to the girl. When the millionaire sobers up, he forgets that he has given the gift, and the tramp is gaoled for the burglary of his house. Much later, the tramp is released from prison, more wretched than ever. The girl is now cured, installed in her own elegant flower shop, and dreaming of the benefactor whom she never saw and whom she imagines must be rich and handsome. The tramp stands outside the shop gazing with joy and adoration, but tries to flee when she approaches him. Giving him a coin and a flower, out of pity, she recognizes the touch of his hand. They gaze at each other. Printed titles convey their words. 'You?' she asks

Chaplin's dissatisfaction with Virginia Cherrill, the leading female role in *City Lights*, stemmed from the fact that she was, in his view, too much of a socialite and did not take her work seriously. In the finished film, however, she looks convincing – thanks perhaps to Chaplin's unrelenting efforts with her.

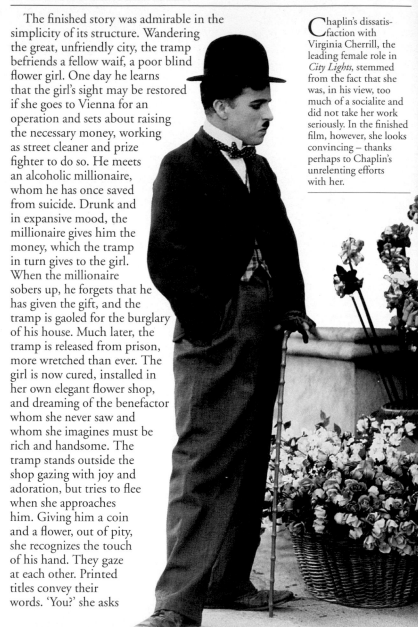

Much of the comic action in *City Lights* revolves around the character of an alcoholic millionaire – played by veteran actor Harry Myers (left). The left-wing writer and dramatist Dan James, who as a young man was Chaplin's assistant on *The Great Dictator*, said: 'He had probably never read Marx, but his conception of the millionaire in *City Lights* is an exact image for Marx's conception of the business cycle.... Chaplin presents a magnificent metaphor. Whether he was aware of the social meaning of this I do not know, but *he got it.*'

in astonishment. He nods. 'You can see now?'

Work on the film was long and difficult. Chaplin was nervous about the talkie revolution and distressed by the death of his mother, in a Hollywood hospital on 28 August 1928, just as he began production. He continued to struggle with new ideas, and was more than usually

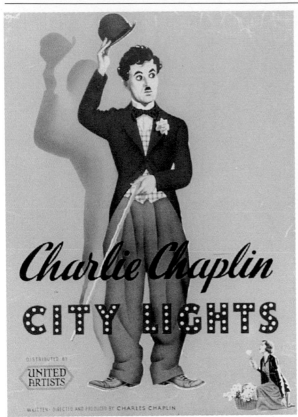

Chaplin's fame spread far and wide. Visitors to his studio, who were duly filmed and photographed for the studio archives, included Winston Churchill (opposite far right), seen on the set of *City Lights* in January 1930. The successive premieres of this film in Los Angeles, New York and London were spectacular occasions. All the Hollywood aristocracy attended the premiere in the brand-new Los Angeles Theater on Broadway, Los Angeles. In New York, Chaplin's guests included Mr and Mrs Albert Einstein (above). In London he sat, somewhat nervously, beside the great Irish playwright George Bernard Shaw (opposite left).

temperamental in his relations with his collaborators: Crocker was among those laid off in the course of the production. At one moment he even sacked Virginia Cherrill, with whom he never formed a particularly cordial relationship; but after making some tests with Georgia Hale, he brought back Cherrill, who took the opportunity to demand a rise in salary.

Sound effects and the musical score

With all the interruptions, shooting continued for twenty-one months. By the end of 1930, when the film was finally edited, every film had to have sound; and *City Lights* was consequently provided with a synchronized track. Chaplin used sound effects very wittily – one outstanding comedy sequence is built around his musical hiccups after he has swallowed a whistle; and in the scene where the statue is unveiled, the voices of the speech-makers are represented by squealing saxophones – a sly dig at the sound quality of many early talkies. Chaplin astonished the film industry and the public by composing the entire musical score for the film

himself. All those who worked with Chaplin on the music of this and subsequent films testify to his melodic skills and his firm ideas of how he wanted the music to sound. Later, his themes for *Modern Times* (1936) and *Limelight* (1952) were to become perennial standards in the popular music repertory.

A world tour

After triumphant premieres in Los Angeles and New York, Chaplin travelled to London for the British premiere and the start of a holiday that was to last

Chaplin acknowledged his debt to the musical arranger in *City Lights*: 'I la-laed and Arthur Johnson wrote it down, and I wish you would give him credit, because he did a very good job.' Later he said, 'I wanted the music to be a counterpoint of grace and charm ... I tried to compose elegant and romantic music to frame my comedies'.

As Chaplin was left-handed, he had to play the violin (below) the other way round.

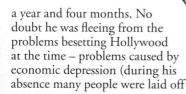

a year and four months. No doubt he was fleeing from the problems besetting Hollywood at the time – problems caused by economic depression (during his absence many people were laid off at the studio, including his loyal cameraman Rollie Totheroh).

In London Chaplin steeled himself to revisit for the first time the school for indigent children at Hanwell, where he had spent a lonely year and a half of his childhood. He thrilled the children with an impromptu performance, but did not keep a promise to visit them again. From Britain he went to Berlin, Vienna, Venice, Paris (where he received the Legion of Honour), the Riviera, Algeria, Spain; then back to Paris and England before finally visiting Singapore and Japan, and returning to Hollywood in June 1932.

During the trip he was fêted by the intellectual and social elite – Winston Churchill, George Bernard Shaw, Albert Einstein, Marlene Dietrich, Aristide Briand, the king of the Belgians, the Prince of Wales, Gandhi and Jean Cocteau. He embarked on a succession of brief romances, one of which was to be touchingly chronicled by the woman involved, May Reeves, in *Charlie Chaplin intime* (1935).

Modern Times: denouncing mechanization

A month after his return to Hollywood he met a twenty-one-year-old divorcée and starlet, Paulette Goddard (whose real name was Pauline Levy). She was to become his wife and the co-star of his next two films.

His world trip had made Chaplin acutely

conscious of the effects of economic depression and the growing dangers of nationalism in Europe. He spent weeks devising a solution to the world economic crisis, and told one newspaper reporter in 1931:

'Unemployment is the vital question.... Machinery should benefit mankind. It should not spell tragedy and throw it out of work.'

No doubt this train of thought influenced his next film *Modern Times*, though he was at pains to emphasize that he was not a propagandist: 'I am always suspicious of a picture with a message'. In his new film, the little tramp, who had begun his life in a very different world, before the First World War, now finds himself one of the millions coping with the new problems of the 1930s – poverty, unemployment, strikes, political intolerance, the tyranny of the machine, narcotics.

In *Modern Times* the tramp is first seen as a factory worker tightening nuts on mysterious components which pass on an endless belt. He goes mad, tightening anything that looks like a nut – even the buttons on the dress of a passing woman.

'Chaplin has always seen the proletarian under the guise of the poor man: hence the broadly human force of his representations but also their political ambiguity. This is quite evident in this admirable film, *Modern Times*, in which he repeatedly approaches the proletarian theme, but never endorses it politically. What he presents us with is the proletarian still blind and mystified, defined by the immediate character of his needs, and his total alienation at the hands of his masters (the employers and the police). For Chaplin, the proletarian is still the man who is hungry; the representations of hunger are always epic with him: excessive size of the sandwiches, rivers of milk, fruit which one tosses aside hardly touched. Ironically, the food-dispensing machine (which is part of the employer's world) delivers only fragmented and obviously flavourless nutriment.'

Roland Barthes
Mythologies, translated
by Annette Lavers, 1972

The film's opening title – 'The story of industry, of individual enterprise – humanity crusading in the pursuit of happiness' – is followed by a symbolic juxtaposition of shots of sheep being herded and of workers streaming out of a factory. The tramp is seen as a worker on a conveyor belt. After getting caught up in the cogs of a giant machine and being used as a guinea pig in an automatic feeding device designed to improve productivity by speeding up lunch times, he runs amok.

In a note about the two main characters in *Modern Times*, Chaplin described the tramp and the woman (played by Paulette Goddard) as: 'The only two live spirits in a world of automatons.'

Hollywood's last silent film: the tramp disappears

Steeling himself to the inevitable, Chaplin actually recorded some dialogue scenes, but then thought better of it. Like *City Lights, Modern Times* was to be essentially a silent film with sound effects and a musical score – again, of course, by Chaplin himself.

At one moment in the film Chaplin's voice is heard, for the first time on screen. When the tramp takes the place of the romantic tenor, he writes the words on his cuffs for easy reference, but the cuffs fly off at his first dramatic gesture. Thus deprived of his prompt, he improvises wonderful gibberish words, of vaguely Italian-like sound, which he sings in a pleasant baritone voice. *Modern Times* was to be Hollywood's last silent film. It also marked the farewell appearance of the tramp.

The last scene of the film (below) shows the couple, arm in arm, heading into the horizon down a country road. 'We'll get along,' says a title.

Journalists and cartoonists had often pointed out the curious coincidence that Chaplin and Hitler – respectively the best loved and the most hated men in the world – were born within four days of each other, in April 1889. Both had chosen to wear similar moustaches, even if only one of them was real. Some even suggested that Hitler had devised his moustache to cash in on Chaplin's popularity. *The Great Dictator* (1940) caused a sensation.

CHAPTER 4

CHAPLIN AFTER THE TRAMP

Chaplin had always been on two sides of the camera. Opposite: in *Limelight*, as an old music hall star. Right: in costume, directing a scene for *The Great Dictator*.

After *Modern Times*, Chaplin recognized that he could no longer ignore talking pictures. Having worked on several projects that eventually came to nothing, including one on the life of Napoleon, Chaplin eventually found, in 1938, a much more fertile subject in the character of Hitler.

The character of Napoleon fascinated Chaplin. In the 1930s he completed two scripts in which he would have played the emperor. He was even photographed in costume for the role (left).

Making fun of 'the homicidal insanity of the Nazis'

Chaplin had become increasingly anguished by what he called, euphemistically, 'a good deal of bad behaviour in the world', and decided that he should endeavour to combat it with his unique weapon – comedy. Later he said that if he had known the full horror of the German concentration camps, he could not have made fun of 'the homicidal insanity of the Nazis'. Fortunately, however, he did so, and the result was *The Great Dictator*.

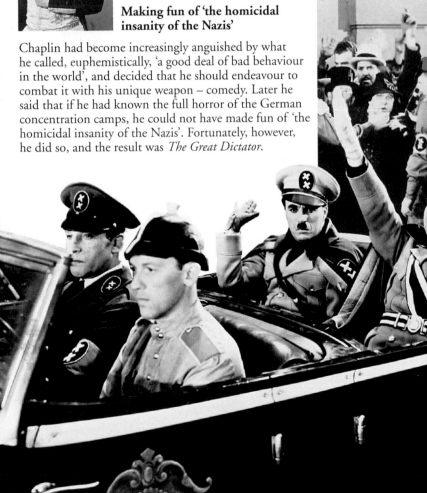

This was to be his first film with dialogue, requiring a revolution in the working methods he had developed since he first began making films. The production of a dialogue film, involving a much larger technical staff brought in from outside, made the old system of taking time off for leisurely conferences on story and gags economically impossible. Chaplin now had to work uninterruptedly, from a definitive script. The old process of reshaping and discarding ideas and gags through discussions was now transferred to the script-writing process. The script for *The Great Dictator* is one of the most elaborate in Hollywood history, running to more than three hundred pages. It is divided into segments, systematically and elaborately identified by letters and numbers.

The Great Dictator: a challenge to the world

From the outset Chaplin had one central idea – the story of a little Jewish barber who accidentally changes places with the monstrous dictator Hynkel whose double he happens to be. The idea of Hynkel's rivalry with the dictator of another country, Benzino Napaloni (an obvious caricature of the Italian Duce, Benito Mussolini), also occurs in early script notes. Although, in hindsight, scenes in which Nazi storm-troopers are treated as slapstick comics make uneasy viewing today, the film contains some of Chaplin's most memorable comic inventions – the little barber's adventures with a great field gun and an aeroplane on the Western front,

In preparing his satire on the dictators Hitler and Mussolini, Chaplin studied newsreel footage of the two men. He wittily parodied the absurd posturing of the Duce – played by Jack Oakie (opposite, next to Chaplin) – the violence against the barber and Hannah – played by Paulette Goddard (above) – and the histrionic oratory of Hitler (overleaf).

where he is left behind when no one informs him the war has ended; Hynkel's eerie ballet with a terrestrial globe. The final speech delivered by the barber when he is thrust in front of a vast political rally, having been mistaken for the dictator, has divided Chaplin's critics. Reactionaries have condemned it as Communist propaganda; radicals have dismissed it as naive. After more than half a century its simple truths are touching.

'Greed has poisoned men's souls – has barricaded the world with hate – has goose-stepped us into misery and bloodshed. We have developed speed, but we have shut ourselves in. Machinery that gives abundance has left us in want. Our knowledge has made us cynical; our cleverness, hard and unkind. We think too much and feel too little. More than machinery we need humanity. More than cleverness we need kindness and goodness. Without these qualities, life will be violent and all will be lost.'

Chaplin ran great risks in making *The Great Dictator* at that juncture in American history. The strength of isolationist and even pro-Fascist feeling in America had discouraged the rest of Hollywood from making overt anti-Nazi subjects. President Roosevelt himself complained that the film could prejudice America's foreign relations. Even though the critical reception was generally favourable – and in wartime Britain, exceptionally enthusiastic – *The Great Dictator* marked the beginning of growing hostility to Chaplin in reactionary America.

The decade following the release of the film in October 1940 was to be the unhappiest in Chaplin's professional and public life.

Hounded by the FBI

Since 1922 J. Edgar Hoover and his Bureau (later Federal Bureau) of Investigation had taken intense interest in Chaplin. He was an alien who had achieved great prominence in Hollywood but had never sought to take American citizenship. The nature of his work tended to attract left-wing intellectuals, and he, for his part, found many of these more interesting than the usual run-of-the-mill Hollywood dinner guests. Chaplin had far too independent a mind to align himself with any political party. Yet, during the hysteria of the 'Red Scares' of the early 1920s and of the Cold War era of the 1940s and 1950s, the authorities went to inordinate, though fruitless, pains to try to demonstrate links between Chaplin and the Communist Party. In May 1942 Chaplin was asked to replace a speaker at a rally in aid of Russian War Relief in San Francisco. From this he acquired a taste for public speaking, and felt he was merely fulfilling his patriotic duty in appearing at meetings for other war causes – in support of the Second Front, of an 'Artists' Front to Win the War', of 'Arts For Russia' and 'Support Our Russian Ally'. FBI agents gleefully monitored Chaplin's every public pronouncement, making much of an occasion when he incautiously addressed his audience as 'comrades'.

The Joan Barry affair

The FBI's activities began to take on much more sinister forms. It fed what appeared to it suitably damaging stories (such as *Pravda*'s approval of *The Pilgrim*, twenty years earlier) to cooperative newspaper columnists. In 1943 an unwitting ally was found in Joan Barry, a young actress whom Chaplin had met in 1941. He was attracted to her physically and seems for a while to have been genuinely convinced that she had possibilities as an actress. However, within less than a year, it became clear that she was mentally unstable and a potential nuisance, if not positively dangerous (she even threatened Chaplin with a gun). Chaplin paid the train fares for her mother to take her to New York. Joan, however, continued to make trouble; and was then taken up as a tool by the FBI.

The FBI orchestrated a series of federal charges, involving Chaplin and others, alleging conspiracy to deprive Miss Barry of her civil rights. A further charge was brought under the Mann Act of 1910, which made it illegal to transport a woman across state lines for immoral purposes – which was the interpretation put upon Chaplin's

The Joan Barry trials resulted from manoeuvres by J. Edgar Hoover and the FBI, deliberately intended to humiliate Chaplin and to bring him into disrepute with the American public. In February 1944 an evidently anguished Chaplin appeared in court in Los Angeles (below and opposite), pushing his way through the photographers. Joan Barry was an unwilling and unreliable witness, and the FBI's efforts to present her drunken and quarrelsome mother in the role of a caring parent are recorded in some of the more amusing episodes in the voluminous files kept on Chaplin by the Bureau.

gift of the train tickets to New York. When these charges variously failed or were withdrawn, the FBI pushed Joan Barry and her mother to bring a paternity case against Chaplin, alleging he was the father of her unborn child. When the child was born, blood tests proved conclusively that Chaplin could not have been the father. However, the Californian courts did not at the time recognize these tests. The first jury failed to agree and

Joan Barry, the state's star witness in the trials of Charles Chaplin (below, with his lawyer, Jerry Giesler), was to become a pitiable figure. After the trials she married and had two more children, but then seems to have separated

were dismissed; a second jury, composed of eleven women and one man, were bludgeoned by the emotional appeals of an old-style, histrionic prosecutor, Joseph Scott, and brought in an 11–1 guilty verdict.

During this sordid process, which dragged on from 1943 to the beginning of 1945, Chaplin met, and, on 16 June 1943 married, Oona O'Neill. She provided him, for the remaining thirty-four years of his life, with the love, companionship and domestic calm that had eluded him.

from her husband, and was committed to mental institutions. After this all trace of her is lost: in the 1990s even her own children did not know whether she was still alive.

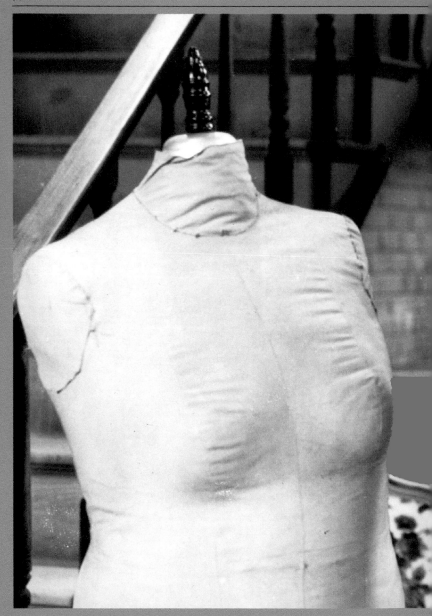

Chaplin called *Monsieur Verdoux* 'a comedy of murders'. The sardonic edge to the film, new to his work, no doubt reflected the disillusionment he felt with post-war America, and the growing intolerance – of which he was one of the most prominent victims – in McCarthy's America. When M. Verdoux is arrested and condemned, he protests that he has only carried to their logical extremes the philosophies of capitalist society. Such views did not exactly endear *Monsieur Verdoux* to the reactionaries of the McCarthy era. In an interview before the film was released, quoted in Theodore Huff, *Charlie Chaplin*, 1951, Chaplin stated: 'The picture has moral value, I believe. Von Clausewitz said that war is the logical extension of diplomacy; M. Verdoux feels that murder is the logical extension of business. He should express the feeling of the times we live in – out of catastrophe come people like him. He typifies the psychological disease and depression. He is frustrated, bitter, and at the end, pessimistic. But he is never morbid; and the picture is by no means morbid in treatment.... Under the proper circumstances, murder can be comic.'

Oona O'Neill was the daughter of the celebrated American playwright Eugene O'Neill. Her parents had separated when she was a small child; and her father publicly voiced his disapproval of the marriage. Their first child Geraldine was born on 1 August 1944; their eighth and last, Christopher, on 8 July 1962.

Monsieur Verdoux

Meanwhile, Chaplin was concentrating on a new film, *Monsieur Verdoux*. In 1942 Orson Welles had suggested the idea of a black comedy about the notorious French wife-murderer, Landru. Subsequently he agreed to assign the idea to Chaplin for a fee of $5000 and the screen credit 'idea suggested by Orson Welles'. Chaplin's scenario is tightly constructed; and the film was shot in a record time, for Chaplin, of three and a half months – from 21 May to 5 September 1946. Paris before the Second World War was reconstructed at the studio, with advice from Chaplin's French associate director, Robert Florey.

Chaplin himself plays the courteous little bank clerk who, having lost his job after the stock market crash, has embarked on a prosperous business of marrying and disposing of rich widows (his admirable supporting cast includes the star comedienne Martha Raye, Isobel Elsom, Margaret Hoffman, Marjorie Bennett and Almira Sessions). Eventually caught, Verdoux stoically goes to the guillotine, questioning the logic of justice in a

Chaplin's associate director on *Monsieur Verdoux* was the French film maker Robert Florey, who no doubt helped to shape Chaplin's characterization of the elegant boulevardier. In the top picture, Verdoux shows no surprise when he is accused by the sister of one of his victims. Before being led to the guillotine (far right), Verdoux is visited by a priest who says, 'May the Lord have mercy on your soul'. 'Why not?' he replies thoughtfully. 'After all, it belongs to him.' Such dialogue was criticized by conservative organizations like the Catholic War Veterans.

society where honest men starve while arms dealers grow rich.

It was irrelevant that the film was set in 1930s France: conservative America of the Cold War Years took the cheerful anarchy of Verdoux's courtroom sentiments all too personally. The original script was modified by the censor, though one line from Verdoux slipped through in the final version of the film: 'One murder makes a villain … millions a hero. Numbers sanctify, my friend.'

A witchhunt in Hollywood

With such ideas, Chaplin had set himself up as a sitting target for America's reactionaries, already stirred up by the FBI's campaign of smears and the Joan Barry trials. At the New York premiere on 11 April 1947 part of the audience was clearly present to demonstrate against the film. The press

conference the next day turned into an inquisition about Chaplin's politics, loyalty and friendships with known Communists like the composer Hanns Eisler.

The opening of *Monsieur Verdoux* coincided with the start of the investigation by the House Un-American Activities Committee into Communist tendencies in the film industry. It was a nightmare period for Hollywood. Chaplin himself was subpoenaed to appear, but the hearing was postponed three times and then abandoned: perhaps the committee had heard of his threat to appear in the tramp costume in order to ridicule the investigation. Fearlessly, he refused to conceal his beliefs and principles, defying the smears of the gossip columnists. When deportation proceedings were begun against Hanns Eisler, Chaplin sent a telegram to Pablo Picasso ('a self-admitted Communist', noted Chaplin's attackers) asking him to organize a protest by French artists to the American embassy in Paris. Gestures like these meant that the Chaplins and their growing family were increasingly isolated in the paranoid film capital.

It is clear that the world, characters and sorrows of *Limelight* were based on the true experiences of Chaplin's own parents. The dominant theme of the fickleness of the public clearly reflected Chaplin's own bitterness about the way so many of his once-adoring audience in America had been persuaded to turn against him by political

and personal vilification. Above left: Chaplin as the eccentric violinist. Opposite: the young Claire Bloom, in the role of the dancer, with Chaplin.

The last appearance of an old clown: *Limelight*

At the height of his troubles with reactionary America, Chaplin made *Limelight*. This film seemed like a nostalgic escape from the uncomfortable reality of late 1940s America to the London and the theatres he had known in his youth.

⟨LIMELIGHT⟩

Chaplin plays Calvero, a once-famous comedian who can no longer find work. In the lodging house where he lives, he saves a young dancer, Terry, from suicide, manages to cure her of psychosomatic

paralysis and helps launch her career. While she becomes the principal dancer at the Empire, Calvero's attempt to make a comeback fails. Terry believes herself in love with her benefactor, who is old enough to be her father; but Calvero disappears from her life, recognizing her real love for a rising young composer, Neville, in whose ballet she dances. Subsequently they meet again. Calvero is given a benefit performance at the Empire and conquers the public once again.

A famous partner

Limelight brought together two of the truly great comedians of the silent cinema Charlie Chaplin and Buster Keaton. Keaton's career had declined since the arrival of sound films and his own subsequent periods of alcoholism. His brilliant comic cameo performance in *Limelight*, however, did much to bring him back to public attention, and to re-establish his reputation – even at the expense of Chaplin's – in his last years. Overleaf: Chaplin as Calvero in a music hall act in which he plays the ringmaster of a flea circus (left); and as a clown in a harlequinade ballet (right).

He has a heart attack and dies in the wings – at the very moment that Terry goes on stage to dance to stardom in Neville's ballet. In the words of the opening title: 'The glamour of Limelight, from which age must fade as youth enters'.

An unforgettable cast

In the role of Terry, Chaplin cast a rising twenty-year-old English actress called Claire Bloom. In other respects the casting was something of a family affair. His two sons by Lita Grey both appeared in the film – twenty-six-year-old Sydney as Neville; and twenty-seven-year-old Charles as a clown in the harlequinade ballet. His three eldest children by Oona, Geraldine, Josephine and Michael, appeared as onlookers in a street scene, in which Geraldine spoke the first line of her acting career. Even Oona appeared briefly, doubling for Claire Bloom. For the ballet sequence, for which he had composed the music, Chaplin engaged two leading New York dancers, André Eglevsky and Melissa Hayden. Especially touching was the casting of the great silent comedian Buster Keaton in the role of Calvero's stage partner in his comedy act. This was the only time the two greatest comics of American silent cinema appeared together; and those who watched them working noted how each tried to outdo the other in comedy, in their roles as an eccentric violinist (Chaplin) and his accompanist.

'I have ... given up my residence in the United States'

Longing to show his wife and children his native country – which inevitably acquired nostalgic charm for him – Chaplin decided to hold the world premiere of Limelight in London. The family set sail on the Queen Elizabeth on 17 September 1952. The ship had been at sea two days when the radio brought the news that the American Attorney-

Chaplin was very anxious about casting the main female role for Limelight. His choice finally fell upon Claire Bloom (below, with Chaplin), a twenty-year-old English actress recommended by the playwright Arthur Laurents, who had seen her acting in London in an adaptation of Jean Anouilh's L'Invitation au château.

General had rescinded Chaplin's re-entry visa. If he attempted to return, the Justice Department said, he could be refused admission under a clause of the alien law barring immigrants on the grounds of 'morals, health or insanity, or for advocating Communism or associating with Communist or pro-Communist organizations'.

Even at the time the authorities knew that if Chaplin chose to come back they would have no case on which to refuse him entry; the FBI files nervously note that his return 'could well rock Immigration and Nationalisation Service and the Department of Justice to its foundations'. They need not have worried.

Chaplin was never again to live in the United States. When in April 1953 he handed over his United States re-entry permit, he stated: 'I have been the object of lies and vicious propaganda by powerful reactionary groups who, by their influence and by aid of America's yellow press, have created an unhealthy atmosphere in which liberal-minded individuals can be singled out and persecuted. Under these conditions I find it virtually impossible to continue my motion picture work, and I have therefore given up my residence in the United States.'

Chaplin is pictured (above) in a happy mood on the deck of the *Queen Elizabeth* on his way from New York to London. It was only his third visit to Europe since he had left Britain in 1913: the last trip had been more than twenty years before. To judge by his expression in the photograph, he was obviously unaware that he would never again return to live in America.

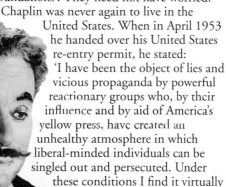

The family settles in Switzerland

Britain welcomed him back as a national

hero, with almost unanimous public condemnation of
America's behaviour. The London premiere of *Limelight*
on 23 October 1952 was a major event and the reviews
of the film as enthusiastic as any Chaplin had ever
received. He delighted in showing his family his native
country, which seemed so safe and friendly after the
America that he had just left. However, income tax in
England was too high to encourage permanent residence.

In January 1953 the Chaplins moved to Switzerland.
The Manoir de Ban, at Corsier-sur-Vevey, was to remain
his home for the rest of his life. Oona, who still retained
an American passport, returned briefly to California to
clear up their financial affairs. In time the house and
studio were sold and Chaplin's final links with the
country that had been his home for almost forty years
were broken.

A deposed and disillusioned king

Deprived of his own studio, Chaplin was determined to
keep on working; he spent 1955 and 1956
preparing a new film, *A King in New York*
(1957). He needed courage to produce it.
Chaplin was accustomed to working in the

security and autonomy of his own studio, with loyal and familiar collaborators. Now he had to rent studio space, work with strangers unaccustomed to his methods, and re-create New York as best he could in London locations. The strain and the handicaps show all too clearly in the finished film; yet it remains a remarkable achievement.

This was the first film that attempted to show the

As he had done for all his films since *City Lights*, Chaplin composed the musical score himself for *A King in New York*, which included some witty parodies of popular songs of the period. Self-taught, he played the violin, cello and piano by ear. Since he played left-handed, his string instruments had to be specially strung in reverse. Overleaf: Chaplin conducting, and demonstrating a melody at the piano, during a recording session for *A King in New York* in 1957.

injustice and paranoia of the political witchhunts in Cold War America. Chaplin brought to bear his strongest weapons – ridicule and pathos. *A King in New York* was released in Europe in autumn 1957. It would not be seen in America until two decades later.

The autobiography of a cinema giant

Even nearing his seventieth birthday, Chaplin could not be idle. He spent 1958 editing a compilation film, *The Chaplin Revue*, comprising *A Dog's Life*, *Shoulder Arms* and *The Pilgrim*, together with sequences showing life at the Hollywood studio at the time these films were made. Chaplin composed and recorded a new musical score for the film. The charming and humorous documentary scenes had been shot in 1918 for

Chaplin's autobiography was translated into at least twenty-five languages. In this joke photograph the Chaplin family pose to show some of the different editions. By this time the two eldest children, Geraldine and Michael, had left home. In descending order of age (from the right) the children are Josephine, Victoria, Eugene, Jane, Annette and Christopher, born in 1962.

a film to be called *How To Make Movies*, which he had abandoned but which was finally assembled in 1981, by Kevin Brownlow and David Gill.

For the next five years, from 1959 to 1964, he was occupied with his autobiography, which he insisted on writing without assistance from 'ghost-writers' or editors. He adopted the method he had used for his scripts, dictating to a secretary, then correcting the typescript extensively in pencil, and giving it back for retyping. This process would be repeated over and over again until he was satisfied with the result. When *My Autobiography* finally appeared in 1964 it was a remarkable work: subsequent research in sources not available at the time to Chaplin reveals that he had an extraordinarily accurate memory. The early part of the book, relating his life up to his entry into films, is far superior to the rest. Clearly childhood sufferings, adolescent ambitions and youthful triumphs were more stimulating to literary creation than an adult life divided between concentrated work, critical adulation, erratic romances and social elevation.

Towards the end of his life, while continuing to spend much of his day working, Chaplin enjoyed spending time with his children, endeavouring to give them the stable family background he had never known. He liked filming them at the Manoir de Ban, their handsome 19th-century mansion set in its own park. Sometimes he would direct them in little improvised dramas. In this photograph (above) taken on the terrace of the Manoir de Ban, where family meals were eaten during the summer, Chaplin films the younger children.

His first film in colour with major stars

By the 1960s the world Chaplin had known was fast disappearing. Edna Purviance had died in 1958 and Mack Sennett in 1960. His brother Sydney followed in 1965, Rollie Totheroh in 1967, and in 1968 Chaplin's eldest son, Charles, aged only forty-three.

The seventy-six-year-old Chaplin announced in 1965 that he was working on a new film called *A Countess from Hong Kong* (1967). Even at this age, he wanted to face new challenges. For the first time in his career he worked for a major distribution company, Universal. With this film he also broke new ground in using colour and CinemaScope, and in employing major international stars – Marlon Brando and Sophia Loren. As in *A Woman of Paris*, more than forty years before, Chaplin himself played only a walk-on role, taking the part of a ship's steward suffering from seasickness.

The filming, which took place in London, became more and more fraught as tension grew between the director and Brando, who could not adapt to Chaplin's way of direction. Chaplin had always preferred actors to reproduce his own personal interpretation of a role, demonstrating how each gesture and line should be done. Moreover, Brando resented Chaplin's authoritarian attitude to his own son, Sydney, who played a supporting role. By the end of shooting any communication between Chaplin and Brando was conducted through the intermediary of the producer, Jerome Epstein.

In 1967 Chaplin completed his last film: *A Countess from Hong Kong*. Despite his age, he showed no sign of slowing down. Although his relations with Sophia Loren (left) were good, her co-star Marlon Brando resented Chaplin's directorial methods.

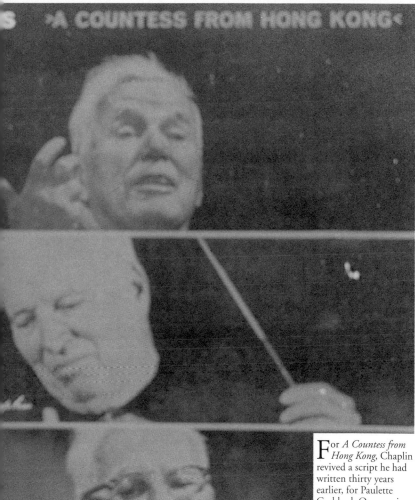

>A COUNTESS FROM HONG KONG<

For *A Countess from Hong Kong*, Chaplin revived a script he had written thirty years earlier, for Paulette Goddard. Once again, Chaplin composed the musical score for his film.

The story was based on an unrealized script written by Chaplin in the 1930s, *Stowaway*. It concerns the adventures of a former White Russian aristocrat working as a Hong Kong taxi-dancer, who hides away in the state cabin of an American ambassador designate.

Panned by the critics

A pleasant romantic comedy, the film seemed positively archaic in the year of *The Graduate* (Mike Nichols), *Bonnie and Clyde* (Arthur Penn), *Belle de Jour* (Luis Bunuel) and *Weekend* (Jean-Luc Godard). The press for the film's London premiere was cruelly unfavourable, though Chaplin was able to take some comfort from a more generous response in continental Europe. Even so, the bitter disappointment of reading some of the worst notices of his career, added to a broken ankle that impaired his hitherto prized agility, finally brought home to Chaplin the inevitability of old age.

Even so, he embarked on a new project, *The Freak*, a dramatic comedy about a young girl who awakes one morning to find that she has sprouted wings. The role was intended for his third daughter, Victoria, who he believed had inherited the gift of comedy to a greater extent than his other children. Even when Victoria left home – to marry and to found, with her husband Jean-Baptiste Thierrée, a travelling circus – Chaplin continued to work on the script, still hoping against hope, to make the film one day.

The last tributes

During the 1970s Chaplin became visibly older and more frail, though the old compulsion to keep on working remained. His very last work was to compose melodies for a new synchronized music track for *A Woman of Paris*; and even though he was by this time unable to walk unaided, he visited the studios to supervise the recording.

In the last years of Chaplin's life the world seemed to compete to pay him homage. In 1971 the Cannes Film

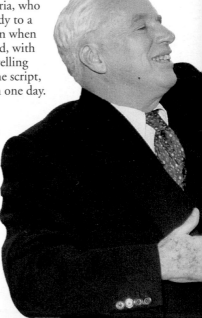

● He was ... one of the greatest comic creators in films, and achieved greater, more widespread fame in his own lifetime than perhaps anyone else in the history of mankind. He ... had to a unique degree the common touch – people of virtually any culture were able to respond with laughter to his screen antics, and for generation after generation of children he was the first introduction to the magic world of cinema. ●
Obituary in *The Times*, December 1977

Festival made a special award for his complete oeuvre and he was invested as Commander of the Legion of Honour. The Venice Biennale honoured him with a special Golden Lion award. In 1975 the Queen knighted him. America was also determined to make amends.

In April 1972 Chaplin was invited to return to Los Angeles to receive a special Academy Award. He had mixed feelings about revisiting America, where he had experienced such triumph and such bitterness, though he was fêted and adored in New York and California. Chaplin was confused and commented – in *My Life in Pictures* (1974) – 'I was touched by the gesture – but there was a certain irony about it somehow'.

After months of failing health, Chaplin died peacefully in the small hours on Christmas Day 1977 at his home in Corsier-sur-Vevey. He was buried in the local churchyard. Yet there was to be one last, macabre joke. His coffin was stolen from the grave by two kidnappers who demanded a ransom. The body was recovered shortly afterwards, in a field not far from his home.

Two decades after his death and sixty years after his character made his last appearance on the screen, the plight of the little tramp is as real as ever. As for Chaplin himself, he remains one of the best loved and most respected comic creators, an acute observer of human nature and the comic possibilities in everyday life, who produced films of dazzling technical virtuosity and unprecedented richness of character.

In 1995, during the Oscar Award Ceremony, *The Guardian* conducted a poll among international cinema critics asking them to name the greatest actor of all. The winner was Charles Chaplin.

In 1972 Chaplin received a special Oscar from Hollywood in recognition of his contribution to the cinema. ' "It was *so emotional* and the *audience – their* emotion. I thought some of them might hiss, but they were so *sweet* – all those famous people, all those artists. You know, they haven't done this to me before. It surpasses everything...." Suddenly summoning that old agility, he flew from his chair. Eyes twinkling, he said, with mock impatience, "Let's go and celebrate, for God's sake!" And happily humming his song "Smile!" he took Oona's arm and stepped out grandly through the door.'

Candice Bergen
Life, 21 April 1972

Overleaf: Chaplin examining *A King in New York* in August 1956.

DOCUMENTS

'Chaplin seemed made for his medium and for no other.
He came to it when he and the films were both young.
He perfected his genius – technique is too poor a word
– with uncanny speed. He was tireless and prolific.
Film after film was produced to delight millions in all
countries.... Fortunately, the film is a permanent medium;
new generations need not take their parents' word
where Chaplin's films are concerned.
They will be able to see for themselves.'

The Times, 27 June 1962

A declaration of the principles of comedy

'What People Laugh At' and 'Pantomime and Comedy' are two articles in which Chaplin reveals the secrets of his art and explains his working methods: how to find gags, how to make the tramp likeable, how to make the emotions of his character felt. Why use dialogue when pantomime is much more effective?

H*is Prehistoric Past*, 1914.

The secrets of laughter

In this text written in 1918, Chaplin explains his techniques for creating comedy: exploiting ridicule, observing scenes from everyday life, constantly striving to create contrasts and surprises.

Comedy moving pictures were an instant success because most of them showed policemen falling down coalholes, slipping into buckets of whitewash, falling off patrol wagons, and getting into all sorts of trouble. Here were men representing the dignity of the law, often very pompous themselves, being made ridiculous and undignified. The sight of their misfortunes at once struck the public funny bone twice as hard as if private citizens were going through like experience.

Even funnier than the man who has been made ridiculous, however, is the man who, having had something funny happen to him, refuses to admit that anything out of the way has happened, and attempts to maintain his dignity. Perhaps the best example is the intoxicated man who, though his tongue and walk give him away, attempts in a dignified manner to convince you that he is quite sober.

He is much funnier than the man who, wildly hilarious, is frankly drunk and doesn't care a whoop who knows it. Intoxicated characters on the stage are almost always 'slightly tipsy' with an attempt at dignity, because theatrical managers have learned that this attempt at dignity is funny.

For this reason, all my pictures are built around the idea of getting me into trouble and so giving me the chance to be desperately serious in my attempt to appear as a normal little gentleman.

That is why, no matter how desperate the predicament is, I am always very much in earnest about clutching my cane, straightening my derby hat, and fixing my tie, even though I have just landed on my head.

I am so sure of this point that I not only try to get myself into embarrassing situations, but I also incriminate the other characters in the picture. When I do this, I always aim for economy of means. By that I mean that when one incident can get two big, separate laughs, it is much better than two individual incidents. In *The Adventurer*, I accomplished this by first placing myself on a balcony, eating ice cream with a girl. On the floor directly underneath the balcony I put a stout, dignified, well-dressed woman at a table. Then, while eating the ice cream, I let a piece drop off my spoon, slip through my baggy trousers, and drop from the balcony onto this woman's neck.

The first laugh came at my embarrassment over my own predicament. The second, and the much greater one, came when the ice cream landed on the woman's neck and she shrieked and started to dance around. Only one incident had been used, but it had got two people into trouble, and had also got two big laughs.

Simple as this trick seems there were two real points of human nature involved in it. One was the delight the average person takes in seeing wealth and luxury in trouble. The other was the tendency of the human being to experience within himself the emotions he sees on the stage or screen.

One of the things most quickly learned in theatrical work is that people as a whole get satisfaction from seeing the rich get the worst of things. The reason for this, of course, lies in the fact that nine tenths of the people in the world are poor, and secretly resent the wealth of the other tenth.

If I had dropped the ice cream, for example, on a scrubwoman's neck, instead of getting laughs, sympathy would have been aroused for the woman. Also, because a scrubwoman has no dignity to lose, that point would not have been funny. Dropping ice cream down a rich woman's neck, however, is, in the minds of the audience, just giving the rich what they deserve.

By saying that human beings experience the same emotions as the people in the incidents they witness, I mean that — taking ice cream as an example — when the rich woman shivered the audience shivered with her. A thing that puts a person in an embarrassing predicament must always be perfectly familiar to an audience, or else the people will miss the point entirely. Knowing that ice cream is cold, the audience shivers. If something was used that the audience did not recognize at once, it would not be able to appreciate the point as well. On this same fact was based the throwing of custard pies in the early pictures. Everyone knew that custard pie is squashy, and so was able to appreciate how the actor felt when one landed on him.

Many persons have asked me where I got the idea for the type of the character I play. Well, all I can say is that it is a composite picture of many Englishmen I had seen in London during the years of my life in that city.

When the Keystone Film Company, with which I made my first pictures, asked me to leave Karno's *Night in an English Music Hall*, a pantomime in which I was playing, I was undecided what to do about the offer, principally because I did not know what kind of a comedy character I could play. Then, after a time, I thought of all the little Englishmen I had seen with small black mustaches, tight-fitting clothes, and bamboo canes, and I decided to model my make-up after these men.

Thinking of the cane was perhaps the best piece of luck I ever had. One reason is that the cane places me, in the minds of the audience, more quickly than anything else could. The other is that I have developed the cane until it has almost a comedy sense of its own. Often, I find it curling itself around someone's leg, or rapping someone on the shoulder and getting a laugh from the audience almost without my knowing that I was directing its action....

Very often I hear a slight ripple at something I had not expected to be funny. At once I prick up my ears and ask myself why that particular thing got a laugh.

In a way, my going to see a movie is really the same as a merchant observing what people are wearing or buying or doing. Anyone who caters to the public has got to keep his knowledge of 'what people like' fresh and up to date.

In the same way that I watch people inside a theater to see when they laugh, I watch them everywhere to get material which they can laugh at.

I was passing a firehouse one day, for example, and heard a fire alarm ring in. I watched the men sliding down the pole, climbing onto the engine, and rushing off to the fire. At once a train of comic possibilities occurred to me. I saw myself sleeping in bed, oblivious to the clanging of the fire bell. This point would have a universal appeal, because everyone likes to sleep. I saw myself sliding down the

pole, playing tricks with the fire hoses, rescuing the heroine, falling off the fire engine as it turned a corner, and many other points along the same lines. I stored these points away in my mind and some time later, when I made *The Fireman*, I used every one of them. Yet if I had not watched the firehouse that day the possibilities in the character of a fireman might never have occurred to me.

Another time, I went up and down a moving staircase in a department store. I got to thinking how this could be utilized for a picture, and I finally made it the basis of *The Floorwalker*. Watching a prize fight suggested *The Champion*, in which I, the small man, knocked out a big bruiser by having a horseshoe concealed in my glove. In another picture I used an employment office as the foundation of the picture. In other words, it has paid me to be always alive to the comic possibilities of the people and the things I see in everyday life.

I was seated in a restaurant once, for example, when I suddenly noticed that a man a few yards away kept bowing and smiling, apparently at me. Thinking he wished to be friendly, I bowed and smiled back at him. As I did this, however, he suddenly scowled at me. I thought I had been mistaken in his intentions. The next minute, however, he smiled again. I bowed; but once more he scowled. I could not imagine why he was smiling and scowling until, looking over my shoulder, I saw he had been flirting with a pretty girl. My mistake made me laugh, and yet it was a natural one on my part. So when the opportunity came a few months ago to utilize such a scene in *A Dog's Life*, I made use of the incident.

Another point about the human being that I use a great deal is the liking of the

T *he Fireman*, 1916.

average person for contrast and surprise in his entertainment. It is a matter of simple knowledge, of course, that the human likes to see the struggle between the good and the bad, the rich and the poor, the successful and the unsuccessful. He likes to cry and he likes to laugh, all within the space of a very few moments. To the average person, contrast spells interest, and because it does, I am constantly making use of it in my pictures.

If I am being chased by a policeman, I always make the policeman seem heavy and clumsy while, by crawling through his legs, I appear light and acrobatic. If I am being treated harshly, it is always a big man who is doing it; so that, by the contrast between big and little, I get the sympathy of the audience, and always I try to contrast my seriousness of manner with the ridiculousness of the incident.

It is my luck, of course, that I am short, and so am able to make these contrasts without much difficulty. Everyone knows that the little fellow in trouble always gets the sympathy of the mob. Knowing that it is part of human nature to sympathize with the 'underdog', I always accentuate my helplessness by drawing my shoulders in, drooping my lip pathetically and looking frightened. It is all part of the art of pantomime, of course. But if I were three inches taller it would be much more difficult to get the sympathy of the audience. I should then look big enough to take care of myself. As it is, the audience, even while laughing at me, is inclined to sympathize with me. As someone once said, it feels like 'mothering me'.

However, one has got to be careful to make the contrast clear enough. At the close of *A Dog's Life*, for example, I am supposed to be a farmer. Accordingly, I thought it might be funny for me to stand in a field, take one seed at a time from my vest pocket, and plant it by digging a hole with my finger. So I told one of my assistants to pick out a farm where this scene could be taken.

Well, he picked out a nice farm; but I did not use it, for the simple reason that it was too small! It did not afford sufficient contrast for my absurd way of planting the seed. It might be slightly funny on a small farm, but done on a large one of about 600 acres, the scene gets a big laugh, simply because of the contrast between my method of planting and the size of the farm.

On almost a par with contrast, I would put surprise.

Surprise has always seemed interesting to me because it is somewhat like news. Whenever I read the newspaper, I am always being surprised at what has happened in the world since yesterday. If, however, before I pick up the newspaper I knew exactly what was going to be in it, I should not be surprised, and therefore not so interested.

I not only plan for surprise in the general incidents of a picture, but I also try to vary my individual actions so that they, too, will come as a surprise. I always try to do the unexpected thing in a novel way. If I think an audience expects me to walk along the street while in a picture, I will suddenly jump on a car. If I want to attract a man's attention, instead of tapping him on the shoulder with my hand or calling to him, I hook my cane around his arm and gently pull him to me.

Figuring out what the audience expects, and then doing something different, is great fun to me. In one of my pictures, *The Immigrant*, the opening scene showed me leaning far over the side of a ship. Only my back could be seen and from the convulsive shudders of my shoulders it looked as though I was seasick. If I had been, it would have been a terrible mistake to show it in the picture. What I was doing was deliberately misleading

the audience. Because, when I straightened up, I pulled a fish on the end of a line into view, and the audience saw that, instead of being seasick, I had been leaning over the side to catch the fish. It came as a total surprise and got a roar of laughter.

There is such a thing, however, as being too funny. There are some plays and pictures at which the audience laughs so much and so heartily that it becomes exhausted and tired. To make an audience roar is the ambition of many actors, but I prefer to spread the laughs out. It is much better when there is a continual ripple of amusement, with one or two big 'stomach laughs', than when an audience 'explodes' every minute or two.

People often ask me if all my ideas work out, and if it is easy to make a funny picture. I sometimes wish they could follow the whole process of getting the idea, working out the characters, taking the film, editing and arranging it.

I am often appalled at the amount of film I have to make in getting a single picture. I have taken as much as 60,000 feet in order to get the 2,000 feet seen by the public. It would take about twenty hours

T*he Immigrant*, 1917.

to run off 60,000 feet on the screen! Yet that amount must be taken to present forty minutes of picture.

Sometimes, when I find that, though I have worked hard over an idea, it has not yet taken final shape in my head, and is therefore not ready to be filmed, I at once drop it and try something else. I do not believe in wasting too much time on something that will not work out. I do believe in concentrating all your energies upon the thing you are doing. But if you can't put it across, after having done your best, try something else for a time, and then come back to your original scheme if you still have faith in it. That is the way I have always worked.

In my work I don't trust anyone's sense of humor but my own. There have been times when the people around the studio have screamed at certain scenes while the picture was in the making, and yet I have discarded those scenes because they did not strike me as being funny enough. It isn't because I think I am so much smarter than those around me. It is simply because I am the one who gets all the blame or credit for the picture. I can't insert a title in a picture, for instance, and say:

'People, I don't blame you for not laughing. I didn't think this was funny myself, but the fellows around me told me it was and so I let it go.'

Here is another point that makes it difficult for me to trust the judgment of those around me. My cameraman and other assistants are so used to me that they don't laugh very much at what I do in rehearsal. If I make a mistake, however, then they laugh. And I, not realizing perhaps that I have made a mistake, am likely to think the scene is funny. I didn't get onto this point until I asked some of them one day why they

The *Immigrant*, 1917.

had laughed at a bit of business that I did not think was amusing. When they told me they had laughed because I had done something wrong, I saw how they might mislead me. So now I am glad they don't always laugh at my stuff.

One of the things I have to be most careful about is not to overdo a thing, or to stress too much any particular point. I could kill laughs more quickly by overdoing something than by any other method. If I made too much of my peculiar walk, if I were too rough in turning people upside down, if I went to excess in anything at all, it would be bad for the picture. Restraint is a great word, not only for actors but for everybody to remember. Restraint of tempers, appetites, desires, bad habits, and so on, is a mighty good thing to cultivate.

One of the reasons I hated the early comedies in which I played was because there couldn't be much 'restraint' in hurling custard pies! One or two custard pies are funny, perhaps; but when nothing but custard pies is used to get laughs, the picture becomes monotonous. Perhaps I do not always succeed by my methods, but I would a thousand times rather get a laugh through something clever and original than through slapstick and horseplay.

There is no mystery connected with 'making people laugh'. All I have ever done is to keep my eyes open and my brain alert for any facts or incidents that I could use in my business. I have studied human nature, because without a knowledge of it I could not do my work. And, as I said at the very beginning of this article, a knowledge of human nature is at the foundation of almost all success.

Charlie Chaplin
'What People Laugh At'
American Magazine, November 1918

A rejection of the talkies

In 1931, when he was working on
City Lights, *Chaplin refused to make a talking picture, arguing that pantomime was a universal language, so there was no need for dialogue.*

Because the silent or nondialogue picture has been temporarily pushed aside in the hysteria attending the introduction of speech [it] by no means indicates that it is extinct or that the motion picture screen has seen the last of it. *City Lights* is evidence of this. In New York it is presented at the George M. Cohan Theater beginning Feb. 6. It is a nondialogue but synchronized film.

Why did I continue to make nondialogue films? The silent picture, first of all, is a universal means of expression. Talking pictures necessarily have a limited field, they are held down to the particular tongue of particular races. I am confident that the future

will see a return of interest in nontalking productions because there is a constant demand for a medium that is universal in its utility. It is axiomatic that true drama must be universal in its appeal – the word elemental might be better – and I believe the medium of presentation should also be a universal rather than a restricted one.

Understand, I consider the talking picture a valuable addition to the dramatic art regardless of its limitations, but I regard it only as an addition, not as a substitute. Certainly it could not be a substitute for the motion picture that has advanced as a pantomimic art form so notably during its brief twenty years of storytelling. After all, pantomime has always been the universal means of communication. It existed as the universal tool long before language was born. Pantomime serves well where languages are in the conflict of a common ignorance. Primitive folk used the sign language before they were able to form an intelligible word.

At what point in the world's history pantomime first made its appearance is speculative. Undoubtedly it greatly antedates the first records of its part in Greek culture. It reached a highly definite development in Rome and was a distinct factor in the medieval mystery plays. Ancient Egypt was adept in its use, and in the sacrificial rites of Druidism and in the war dances of the aborigines of all lands it had a fixed place.

Pantomime lies at the base of any form of drama. In the silent form of the photoplay it is the keynote. In the vocal form it must always be an essential, because nonvisual drama leaves altogether too much to the imagination. If there is any doubt of this, an example is the radio play.

C*ity Lights*, 1931.

I am a comedian and I know that pantomime is more important in comedy than it is in pure drama. It may be even more effective in farce than in straight comedy. These two differ in that the former implies the attainment of humor without logical action – in fact, rather the reverse; and the latter achieves this attainment as the outcome of sheer legitimate motivation. Silent comedy is more satisfactory entertainment for the masses than talking comedy, because most comedy depends on swiftness of action, and an event can happen and be laughed at before it can be told in words. Of course, pantomime is invaluable in drama, too, because it serves to effect the gradual transition from farce to pathos or from comedy to tragedy much more smoothly and with less effort than speech can ever do.

Action is more generally understood than words. The lift of an eyebrow, however faint, may convey more than a hundred words. Like the Chinese symbolism, it will mean different things, according to its scenic connotation. Listen to a description of some unfamiliar object – an African warthog, for example – then describe it; observe a picture of the animal and then note the variety of astonishment.

We hear a great deal about children not going to the movies any more, and it is undoubtedly true that hundreds of thousands of prospective film patrons, of future film-goers, young tots who formerly thrilled to the silent screen, do not attend any more because they are unable to follow the dialogue of talking pictures readily. On the other hand, they do follow action unerringly. This is because the eye is better trained than the ear. There is nothing in *City Lights* that a child won't follow easily and understand.

I base this statement on recent observations; the sudden arrival of dialogue in motion pictures is causing many of our actors to forget the elementals of the art of acting. Pantomime, I have always believed and still believe, is the prime qualification of a successful screen player. A truly capable actor must possess a thorough grounding in pantomime. Consider the Irvings, Coquelins, Bernhardts, Duses, Mansfields, and Booths, and you will find at the root of their art pantomime.

My screen character remains speechless from choice. *City Lights* is synchronized and certain sound effects are part of the comedy, but it is a nondialogue picture because I preferred that it be that, for the reasons I have given.

Charlie Chaplin
'Pantomime and Comedy'
The New York Times
25 January 1931

My Autobiography

Between 1959 and 1964, Charlie Chaplin set about writing his autobiography. While he was in his seventies, he dipped back into his memories and traced the different stages of his long career. From the first appearance of the tramp and the phenomenal success he experienced immediately after, to the happiness of his final years: extracts from a busy life.

T he tramp's shoes.

Taking on the role of tramp

In January 1914, when Chaplin had been at the Keystone studios for a few months, Mack Sennett asked Chaplin to come up with some new ideas for gags. It was at this time that Chaplin invented the character of the tramp.

I was in my street clothes and had nothing to do, so I stood where Sennett could see me. He was standing with Mabel, looking into a hotel lobby set, biting the end of a cigar. 'We need some gags here,' he said, then turned to me. 'Put on a comedy make-up. Anything will do.'

I had no idea what make-up to put on. I did not like my get-up as the press reporter. However, on the way to the wardrobe I thought I would dress in baggy pants, big shoes, a cane and a derby hat. I wanted everything a contradiction: the pants baggy, the coat tight, the hat small and the shoes large. I was undecided whether to look old or young, but remembering Sennett had expected me to be a much older man, I added a small moustache, which, I reasoned, would add age without hiding my expression.

I had no idea of the character. But the moment I was dressed, the clothes and the make-up made me feel the person he was. I began to know him, and by the time I walked on to the stage he was fully born. When I confronted Sennett I assumed the character and strutted about, swinging my cane and parading before him. Gags and comedy ideas went racing through my mind.

The secret of Mack Sennett's success was his enthusiasm. He was a great audience and laughed genuinely at what he thought funny. He stood and giggled until his body began to shake. This encouraged me and I began to explain the character: 'You know this fellow is many-sided, a tramp, a gentleman, a poet, a dreamer, a lonely fellow, always hopeful of romance and adventure. He would have you believe he is a scientist, a musician, a duke, a polo-player. However, he is not above picking up cigarette-butts or robbing a baby of its candy. And, of course, if the occasion warrants it, he will kick a lady in the rear – but only in extreme anger!'

I carried on this way for ten minutes or more, keeping Sennett in continuous chuckles. 'All right,' said he, 'get on the set and see what you can do there.'...

In all comedy business an attitude is most important, but it is not always easy to find an attitude. However, in the hotel lobby I felt I was an impostor posing as one of the guests, but in reality I was a tramp just wanting a little shelter. I entered and stumbled over the foot of a lady. I turned and raised my hat apologetically, then turned and stumbled over a cuspidor, then turned and raised my hat to the cuspidor. Behind the camera they began to laugh.

Quite a crowd had gathered there, not only the players of the other companies who left their sets to watch us, but also the stage-hands, the carpenters and the wardrobe department. That indeed was a compliment. And by the time we had finished rehearsing we had quite a large audience laughing. Very soon I saw Ford Sterling [a Keystone comedian] peering over the shoulders of the others. When it was over I knew I had made good....

Charles Chaplin
My Autobiography, 1964

Charlie and Sydney Chaplin on the set of *The Immigrant*, 1917.

Dealing with success

When he was taken on by the Essanay company in 1915, Chaplin became an instant success. The image of the tramp appeared everywhere....

My success had taken on such proportions that Sydney now intended devoting his whole time to my business affairs. According to reports, my popularity kept increasing with each succeeding comedy. Although I knew the extent of my success in Los Angeles by the long lines at the box-office, I did not realise to what magnitude it had grown elsewhere. In New York, toys and statuettes of my character were being sold in all the department stores and drugstores. Ziegfeld Follies Girls were doing Chaplin numbers, marring their beauty with moustaches, derby hats, big shoes and baggy trousers, singing a song called *Those Charlie Chaplin Feet*.

We were also inundated with all manner of business propositions involving books, clothes, candles, toys, cigarettes and toothpaste.

Also stacks upon stacks of increasing fanmail became a problem. Sydney insisted that it should all be answered, in spite of the expense of having to engage an extra secretary....

Charles Chaplin
My Autobiography, 1964

Humour

I did not have to read books to know that the theme of life is conflict and pain. Instinctively, all my clowning was based on this. My means of contriving comedy plot was simple. It was the process of getting people in and out of trouble....

My own concept of humour is ... the subtle discrepancy we discern in what appears to be normal behaviour. In other words, through humour we see in what seems rational, the irrational; in what seems important, the unimportant. It also heightens our sense of survival and preserves our sanity. Because of humour we are less overwhelmed by the vicissitudes of life. It activates our sense of proportion and reveals to us that in an over-statement of seriousness lurks the absurd.

For instance, at a funeral where friends and relatives are gathered in hushed reverence around the bier of the departed, a late arrival enters just as the service is about to begin and hurriedly tiptoes to his seat, where one of the mourners has left his top hat. In his hurry, the late arrival accidentally sits on it, then with a solemn look of mute apology, he hands it crushed to its owner, who takes it with mute annoyance and continues listening to the service. And the solemnity of the moment becomes ridiculous.

Charles Chaplin
My Autobiography, 1964

'A few remarks about film-making'

Personally, I loathe tricky effects, photographing through the fireplace from the viewpoint of a piece of coal, or travelling with an actor through a hotel lobby as though escorting him on a bicycle; to me they are facile and obvious. As long as an audience is familiar with the set, it does not want the tedium of a travelling smear across the screen to see an actor move from one place to another. Such pompous effects slow up action, are boring and unpleasant, and have been mistaken for that tiresome word 'art'.

My own camera set-up is based on facilitating choreography for the actor's movements. When a camera is placed on the floor or moves about the player's nostrils, it is the camera that is giving the performance and not the actor. The camera should not obtrude.

Time-saving in films is still the basic virtue. Both Eisenstein and Griffith knew it. Quick cutting and dissolving from one scene to another are the dynamics of film technique....

In handling actors in a scene, psychology is most helpful. For instance a member of the cast may join the company in the middle of a production. Although an excellent actor he may be nervous in his new surroundings. This is where a director's humility can be very helpful, as I have often found under these circumstances. Although knowing what I wanted, I would take the new member aside and confide in him that I was tired, worried and at a loss to know what to do with the scene. Very soon he would forget his own nervousness and try to help me and I would get a good performance out of him....

Charles Chaplin
My Autobiography, 1964

A fulfilled man at the end of his life

Chaplin reflects on his extraordinary life and on the happiness his family (below, in 1961) has given him.

So now I shall end this Odyssey of mine. I realise that time and circumstances have favoured me. I have been cosseted in the world's affections, loved and hated. Yes, the world has given me its best and little of its worst. Whatever were my ill vicissitudes, I believe that fortune and ill-fortune drift upon one haphazardly as clouds. Knowing this, I am never too shocked at the bad things that happen and am agreeably surprised at the good. I have no design for living, no philosophy – whether sage or fool, we must all struggle with life. I vacillate with inconsistencies; at times small things will annoy me and catastrophes will leave me indifferent.

Nevertheless, my life is more thrilling today than it ever was. I am in good health and still creative and have plans to produce more pictures – perhaps not with myself, but to write and direct them for members of my family – some of whom have quite an aptitude for the theatre. I am still very ambitious; I could never retire. There are many things I want to do; besides having a few unfinished cinema scripts, I should like to write a play and an opera – if time will allow.

Schopenhauer said happiness is a negative state – but I disagree. For the last twenty years I have known what happiness means. I have the good fortune to be married to a wonderful wife. I wish I could write more about this, but it involves love, and perfect love is the most beautiful of all frustrations because it is more than one can express....

With such happiness, I sometimes sit out on our terrace at sunset and look over a vast green lawn to the lake in the distance, and beyond the lake to the reassuring mountains, and in this mood think of nothing and enjoy their magnificent serenity.

Charles Chaplin
My Autobiography, 1964

The execution of a brilliant humorist

'Rhythm' was written by Chaplin in 1938, on the eve of the Second World War. It relates the story of a condemned man awaiting his execution in a prison courtyard. In the piece Chaplin the writer-film maker is preoccupied with justice – and with injustice. A year later, he started shooting The Great Dictator, *a call to all people of good will.*

The Great Dictator, 1940.

Only the dawn moved in the stillness of that small Spanish prison yard – the dawn ushering in death, as the young Loyalist stood facing the firing squad. The preliminaries were over. The small group of officials had stepped to one side to witness the end, and now the scene had tightened into ominous silence.

Up to the last, the Rebels had hoped that a reprieve would come from headquarters, for although the condemned man was an enemy to their cause, in the past he had been a popular figure in Spain, a brilliant writer of humor, who had contributed much to the enjoyment of his fellow country-men.

The officer in charge of the firing squad knew him personally. Before the Civil War they had been friends. Together they had been graduated from the university in Madrid. Together they had worked for the overthrow of the monarchy and the power of the Church. And together they had caroused, had sat at nights around café tables, had laughed and joked, had enjoyed evenings of metaphysical discussion. At times they had argued on the dialectics of government. Their technical differences were friendly then, but now those differences had wrought misery and upheaval over all Spain and had brought his friend to die by the firing squad.

But why think of the past? Why reason? Since the Civil War what good was reason? In the silence of the prison yard these interrogative thoughts ran feverishly through the officer's mind.

No. He must shut out the past. Only the future mattered. The future? A world in which he would be deprived of many old friends.

That morning was the first time they had met since the war. But never a word was spoken. Only a faint smile of recognition passed between them as they prepared for the march into the prison yard.

From the sombre dawn streaks of silver and red peered over the prison wall and breathed a quiet requiem in rhythm with the stillness in the yard, a rhythm pulsating in silence like the throbbing of a heart. Out of that silence the voice of the commanding officer resounded against the prison walls. 'Attention!'

At this command six subordinates snapped their rifles to their sides and stiffened. The unity of their action was followed by a pause in which the next command was to be given.

But in that pause something happened, something that broke the line of rhythm. The condemned man coughed and cleared his throat. This interruption broke the concatenation of procedure.

The officer turned, expecting the prisoner to speak, but no words came. Turning to his men again, he was about to proceed with the next command, but a sudden revolt took possession of his brain, a psychic amnesia that left his mind a blank. He stood bewildered before his men. What was the matter? The scene in the prison yard had no meaning. He saw only objectively – a man with his back to the wall facing six others. And the group there on the side, how foolish they looked, like rows of clocks that had suddenly stopped ticking. No one moved. No one made sense. Something was wrong. It must all be a dream, and he must snap out of it.

Dimly his memory began to return. How long had he been standing there? What had happened? Ah, yes! He had issued an order. But what order came next?

Following 'attention' was the command, 'present arms', and after that, 'to aim', and then 'fire'! A faint concept of this was in the back of his mind. But words to utter it seemed far off – vague and outside himself.

In this dilemma he shouted incoherently, jumbled words that had no meaning. But to his relief the men presented arms. The rhythm of their action set his brain in rhythm, and again he shouted. Now the men took aim.

But in the pause that followed, there came into the prison yard hurrying footsteps the nature of which the officer knew meant a reprieve. Instantly his mind cleared. 'Stop!' he screamed frantically at the firing squad.

Six men stood poised with rifles. Six men were caught in rhythm. Six men when they heard the scream to stop – fired.

Charlie Chaplin
'Rhythm: A Story of Men in Macabre Movement' in
The Best of Rob Wagner's Script, edited by Anthony Slide, 1985

Fellow comedians and film directors have their say

From Stan Laurel to Buster Keaton, from Jacques Tati to Howard Hawks, many people have paid homage to Charlie Chaplin: his professionalism, verging on the pernickety, his great sense of timing, the tragic dimension of his tramp character and his ability to display extreme emotion.

Chaplin's professionalism

The French comedian Max Linder, who was said to have been Chaplin's inspiration and model, recounts the meticulous work that went into Chaplin's films.

When you see a film by Charlie Chaplin, it is easy to recognize the amount of work it represents. Even so, however well informed one is, it would be impossible to conceive the continuous and highly intelligent effort of Charlie Chaplin.

Chaplin has wanted to assure me that it was seeing my films that inspired him to work in the cinema. He calls me his teacher, but I have been the happy one, to take lessons in his school. A lot of nonsense has been talked about Chaplin. First of all, he is English in origin and not French or Spanish as has been said. It was I who first told him that in France he was called Charlot and his brother Sydney, Julot. They were vastly amused by this, and spent the day calling each other these names, with great bursts of laughter. Charlie has been a performer since he was a child. He is a remarkable musician and composer.

Chaplin has built his own studio in Los Angeles, where he makes his films himself, with the collaboration of his brother and a dozen assistants for the production. Charlie directs with the most minute care. His studio, of course, is equipped with all the most modern improvements, conveniences and apparatus. But the secret does not lie in the mechanical work. It is in the method. Charlie, as a true humorist, has studied laughter, and has achieved

Charlie Chaplin and Max Linder, c. 1921.

a rare precision in evoking it. He leaves nothing to the chance of improvization. He rehearses every scene until he is absolutely satisfied with it. He films every rehearsal and projects them several times, in order to pick out any fault or imperfection that could prejudice the effect he is seeking. He starts over again until he is satisfied, and he is himself harder to please than the most harshly critical of his spectators.

Max Linder in *Le Film*, 1919
Translated in David Robinson
Chaplin: The Mirror of Opinion, 1983

Mack Sennett, the head of the Keystone studios, remembers Chaplin at the start of his career, when he was working for Keystone in 1914. The actor was demanding, painstaking and always present.

Of all the people I knew, he was the person who was the most focused on what concerned him – his future, the sort of thing he was attempting to do. He wanted to work – and nearly all the time.... He was always complaining about this or that or something else – about the director he had, about the sort of actors who worked with him, about the fact that his role was not big enough, or that he needed more space on set to do what he had to do and how he wanted to do it. And when the moment came for the first showing of the film, he was always present, while the majority of actors in the film stayed away. If he did not like something while the film was being shown, he clicked his tongue and his fingers, he fidgeted and moved about restlessly.

Mack Sennett
Conversation related by
Theodore Dreiser, August 1928

Making a Living, Chaplin's first film (1914). Chaplin had not yet adopted the role of the tramp.

Chaplin's fellow comedian Buster Keaton has often been compared to Charlie Chaplin. Here Keaton talks about Chaplin's attention to detail.

I must admit that Charlie is, in private, the most cheerful and the most thoughtful companion. To tell the truth, it was when he was working that he was less funny, if I may say so. Calm, cold, lucid, attentive, he pushed his love of perfection to the limit, becoming as meticulous as a collector handling the wings of a butterfly.

One never ceases to be amazed at his skill in the use of detail, at the clockwork way his films unfold, which is, possibly, the essence of his genius, more important than his ability to come up with gags, because it is through this perfect precision that his comic sense is moulded into eternal material: into the human form itself.

Buster Keaton
Arts, 3 October 1952

The comedian Stan Laurel, who also worked for Fred Karno's Companies, emphasized Chaplin's singlemindedness.

The difference between Charlie and all the rest of us who made comedy – with only one exception, Buster Keaton – was that he just absolutely refused to do anything but the best. To get the best he worked harder than anyone I know.

Stan Laurel
in John McCabe
Charlie Chaplin, 1978

A wide appeal

The French poet, novelist and film maker Jean Cocteau grasped the richness of the burlesque in Chaplin's work. There is something of interest in it for everyone: subtlety of effects or an explosion of gags.

Chaplin is the modern clown – he speaks to all ages, to all people. A sort of Esperanto laughter. Everyone looks for amusement in his work for different reasons. No doubt, with his help, the Tower of Babel would have been completed. He never overdoes any of the effects that he is constantly finding; people with quick minds enjoy those, while others are satisfied with his larking around.

Jean Cocteau
Carte blanche, 1919

A child's outlook

The influential Russian theatre and film director Sergei Eisenstein took a close interest in Chaplin, seeing in him the

symbol of both freedom and rebellion against war or ultramodernism.

One of Chaplin's *characteristics* is that in spite of his grey hair he has preserved a 'child's outlook' on life and spontaneous perception of events.

Hence his freedom from the 'fetters of morals' and his ability to see as comic things which make other people's flesh creep.

Such a trait in an adult is known as infantilism.

Hence Chaplin's comic constructions are based chiefly on an infantile method....

Reality itself brings grist to Chaplin's mill.

Chaplin sees war as a bloody incongruity in *Shoulder Arms*.

He sees the new era of our day in *Modern Times*.

It is not true that Chaplin's partner is a terrible-looking, tall, strong and ruthless fat man who runs a Hollywood restaurant when he is free from his work at the studios.

Charlie Chaplin on the set of *Monsieur Verdoux* in 1946.

In all his repertoire Chaplin has another partner, still taller, still more terrible, still stronger and still more ruthless. With this partner – reality – Chaplin performs an endless series of circus stunts for us. Reality is like a grim 'white-faced clown'. It seems wise and logical, prudent and far-seeing. But in the end it is fooled, ridiculed. Its guileless and childlike partner, Chaplin, gains the upper hand. He laughs in a carefree manner, without realizing that his laughter is a verdict on reality.

Sergei Eisenstein, 'Charlie the Kid', *Notes of a Film Director*, trans X. Danko, 1959

Monsieur Verdoux and our time

The French writer and film director, Jean Renoir, defended Charlie Chaplin's new look in Monsieur Verdoux.

It is agreed, some will say, that Chaplin has created a highly personal work, and we admit that he has undergone a natural artistic transformation.

We only feel that he has done all this in a wrong direction. And they add that the greatest crime of *Monsieur Verdoux* was the killing-off of the beloved little vagabond who had been such a charmer. His creator should not only have kept him alive but depended on him in his search for a new form of expression. I cannot share this opinion.

In giving up the rundown shoes, the old derby hat and willowy cane of the raggedy little guy whose pathetic hangdog look used to melt our hearts, Chaplin has gone deliberately into a world that is more dangerous, because it is closer to the one we live in. His new character, with neatly-pressed trousers, impeccably-knotted tie, well-dressed and no longer able to appeal to our pity, does not belong in those good old situations, outlined in strong broad strokes, where the rich trample the poor in so obvious a manner that even the most childish audience can immediately grasp the moral of the story. Before, we could imagine that the adventures of the little tramp took place in some world that belonged exclusively to the movies, that they were a sort of fairy tale.

With *Monsieur Verdoux*, such misapprehension is no longer possible. This one really takes place in our time, and the problems faced on the screen are really our own. By thus giving up a formula which afforded him full security, and undertaking squarely the critique of the society in which he himself lives, a dangerous job if ever there was one, the author raises our craft to the level of the great classical expressions of the human novel, and strengthens our hope of being able to look upon it more and more as an art.

Jean Renoir
'Chaplin Among the Immortals'
in *Screen Writer*, July 1947

Buster Keaton and Charlie Chaplin with Alf Reeves, Chaplin's studio manager.

Buster Keaton on the early silent days and Chaplin's popularity

We worked hard. We stayed with the story all of the way. In the old days all of us – Chaplin, Lloyd, Harry Langdon, and myself – worked with our writers from the day they started on a story. We checked on the scenery, the cast, the locations – often going on trips with the unit manager to pick these out ourselves and make sure they were suitable. We directed our own pictures, making up our own gags as we went along, saw the rushes, supervised the cutting, went to the sneak previews.... We were the ones who decided what should go into a script to make the audience laugh....

No comedian ever has been so worshipped around the world as Chaplin was in those years.... At his best, and Chaplin remained at his best for a long time, he was the greatest comedian that ever lived.... I was always puzzled later on when people spoke of the similarities in the characters Charlie and I played in movies. There was, to me, a basic difference from the start: Charlie's tramp was a bum with a bum's philosophy. Lovable as he was he would steal if he got the chance. My little fellow was a working man and honest.

Buster Keaton with Charles Samuels
My Wonderful World of Slapstick, 1967

The tramp and Monsieur Hulot

The French film director Jacques Tati acknowledges his debt to Chaplin.

Without him I would never have made a film. With Keaton he was the master of us all. His work is always contemporary, yet eternal, and what he brought to the cinema and to his time is irreplaceable.

Jacques Tati
Quoted in David Robinson
Chaplin: His Life and Art, 1985

The sequence shot and cinéma-vérité

The Nouvelle Vague *director Jean-Luc Godard sees in Chaplin a human film maker, an inventor, a free man.*

He is above all praise because he is the greatest. Why say otherwise? In any case he is the only film maker who can bear the misleading term human, without any misunderstanding. From the invention of the sequence shot in *The Champion* to that of cinéma-vérité in the final speech of *The Great Dictator*, Charles Spencer Chaplin, while staying on the fringe of the cinema, has finally filled this fringe with more things (what else can one call them: ideas, gags, intelligence, humour, beauty, gestures?) than all film makers....

Today people say 'Chaplin' as they say 'da Vinci', or rather 'the tramp' as they say 'Leonardo'. And what better homage, in the 20th century, to give an artist of the cinema than to quote the words of Rossellini after seeing *A King in New York*: 'It is the film of a free man.'

Jean-Luc Godard
in *Les Cahiers du cinéma*, 1964

T*he Great Dictator*, 1940.

The only film maker to have known hunger

For the French director François Truffaut, the films with the tramp are all the more moving as they were created from the childhood of the film maker.

Charlie Chaplin, abandoned by his alcoholic father, lived his early years in the fear of seeing his mother taken away to the mental asylum, then, when she was taken there, in the fear of being rounded up by the police; it was a little tramp of nine years old who hugged the walls of Kennington Road, living, as he said in his autobiography, 'in the lower strata'. If I go back over this childhood

which has been described and commented on so often that people might have forgotten how harsh it was, it is only so that one can see what an explosive mixture there is in dire poverty. When Chaplin joined Keystone to make films featuring chases, he ran faster and further than his music-hall colleagues because, even if he is not the only film maker to have described hunger, he is the only one to have known it, and the whole world felt that when the first film reels started to turn from 1914.

François Truffaut
Preface to André Bazin
Charlie Chaplin, 1988

Comedy and tragedy

The great American director Howard Hawks acknowledges Chaplin's influence.

In the first place, true drama is awfully close to being comedy. The greatest drama in the world is really funny. A man who loses his pants out in front of a thousand people – he's suffering the tortures of the damned, but he's awfully funny doing it. I had a damn good teacher, Chaplin. Probably our greatest comic. And everything he did was tragedy. He made things funny out of tragedy. I work a lot on that. I wanted to do *Don Quixote* with Cary Grant and Cantinflas, and people said, 'But that isn't comedy – that's a tragedy.' I'd have to go into a long explanation. I think we could have a lot of fun with it. I think that Don Quixote's the basis really for the Chaplin character.... I like Keaton's [films]. But Chaplin is the best of 'em all.

Joseph McBride
Hawks on Hawks, 1982

FILMOGRAPHY

Note: The system of numbering in this filmography is the one established in Uno Asplund, *Chaplin's Films* (1971) and subsequently followed by other works on Chaplin.

THE KEYSTONE FILMS

Production: the Keystone Film Company.
Producer: Mack Sennett. Unless otherwise stated, writer and director: Charles Chaplin.

1914

1 *Making a Living*
  Director: Henry Lehrman
2 *Kid Auto Races at Venice*
  Director: Henry Lehrman
3 *Mabel's Strange Predicament*
  Directors: Henry Lehrman, Mack Sennett
4 *Between Showers*
  Director: Henry Lehrman
5 *A Film Johnnie*
  Director: George Nichols
6 *Tango Tangles*
  Director: Mack Sennett
7 *His Favorite Pastime*
  Director: George Nichols
8 *Cruel, Cruel Love*
  Director: George Nichols
9 *The Star Boarder*
  Director: George Nichols
10 *Mabel at the Wheel*
  Directors: Mabel Normand, Mack Sennett
11 *Twenty Minutes of Love*
12 *Caught in a Cabaret*
  Director: Mabel Normand
13 *Caught in the Rain*
14 *A Busy Day*
15 *The Fatal Mallet*
  Director: Mack Sennett
16 *Her Friend the Bandit*
  Director: unknown
17 *The Knockout*
  Director: Charles Avery
18 *Mabel's Busy Day*
  Director: Mabel Normand
19 *Mabel's Married Life*
20 *Laughing Gas*
21 *The Property Man*
22 *The Face on the Bar Room Floor*
23 *Recreation*
24 *The Masquerader*

25 *His New Profession*
26 *The Rounders*
27 *The New Janitor*
28 *Those Love Pangs*
29 *Dough and Dynamite*
30 *Gentlemen of Nerve*
31 *His Musical Career*
32 *His Trysting Place*
33 *Tillie's Punctured Romance*
  Director: Mack Sennett
34 *Getting Acquainted*
35 *His Prehistoric Past*

THE ESSANAY FILMS

Production: the Essanay Film Manufacturing Company
Producer: Jesse T. Robbins. Writer and director: Charles Chaplin.
Photography (except *His New Job*): Harry Ensign.
Leading female role in all films except *His New Job*: Edna Purviance

1915

36 *His New Job*
37 *A Night Out*
38 *The Champion*
39 *In the Park*
40 *A Jitney Elopement*
41 *The Tramp*
42 *By the Sea*
43 *Work*
44 *A Woman*
45 *The Bank*
46 *Shanghaied*
47 *A Night in the Show*

1916

48 *Charlie Chaplin's Burlesque on Carmen*
49 *Police*
50 *Triple Trouble*
  (compilation unauthorized by Chaplin)

THE MUTUAL FILMS

Production: Chaplin's Lone Star Studio for release by the Mutual Film Corporation.
Producer, writer and director: Charles Chaplin.
Photography: Frank D.Williams (*The Floorwalker*, *The Fireman*, *The Vagabond*), Roland Totheroh (all others).

Leading female role except in *One A.M*:
Edna Purviance

1916

51 *The Floorwalker*
52 *The Fireman*
53 *The Vagabond*
54 *One A.M.*
55 *The Count*
56 *The Pawnshop*
57 *Behind the Screen*
58 *The Rink*

1917

59 *Easy Street*
60 *The Cure*
61 *The Immigrant*
62 *The Adventurer*

THE FIRST NATIONAL FILMS

Production: the Chaplin Studio for release
by First National Exhibitors' Circuit.
Producer, writer and director: Charles Chaplin.
Photography: Roland Totheroh.
Leading female role in all films: Edna Purviance

1918

63 *A Dog's Life*
64 *The Bond*
65 *Shoulder Arms*

1919

66 *Sunnyside*
67 *A Day's Pleasure*

1921

68 *The Kid*
69 *The Idle Class*

1922

70 *Pay Day*
71 *The Pilgrim*

THE UNITED ARTISTS FILMS

Production: the Chaplin Studio for release by
United Artists.
Producer, writer and director: Charles Chaplin.
Photography: Roland Totheroh (to *Modern Times*)

1923

72 *A Woman of Paris*
      with Edna Purviance, Adolphe Menjou

1925

73 *The Gold Rush*
      with Georgia Hale

1928

74 *The Circus*
      with Merna Kennedy

1931

75 *City Lights*
      with Virginia Cherrill

1936

76 *Modern Times*
      with Paulette Goddard

1940

77 *The Great Dictator*
      with Paulette Goddard
Photography: Karl Struss, Roland Totheroh

1947

78 *Monsieur Verdoux*
      with Marilyn Nash, Martha Raye
Photography: Curt Courant, Roland Totheroh

1952

79 *Limelight*
      with Claire Bloom, Buster Keaton,
      Sydney Chaplin
Photography: Karl Struss

BRITISH PRODUCTIONS

1957

80 *A King in New York*
      with Dawn Addams
Production: Attica-Archway
Photography: Georges Périnal

1967

81 *A Countess from Hong Kong*
      with Sophia Loren, Marlon Brando
Production: Universal Pictures
Photography: Arthur Ibbetson

FURTHER READING

Barthes, Roland, *Mythologies*, 1957

Chaplin, Charles, *My Autobiography*, 1964

—, *My Early Years*, 1979

—, *My Life in Pictures*, 1974

Chaplin, Charles Spencer, Jr., *My Father, Charlie Chaplin*, 1960

Clair, René, *Reflections on the Cinema*, 1953

Delluc, Louis, *Charlie Chaplin*, trans. Hamish Miles, 1922

Haining, Peter (ed.), *Charlie Chaplin: A Centenary Celebration*, 1989

Huff, Theodore, *Charlie Chaplin*, 1951

McBride, Joseph, *Hawks on Hawks*, 1982

McCabe, John, *Charlie Chaplin*, 1978

MacCaffrey, Donald William, *Four Great Comedians: Chaplin, Lloyd, Keaton, Langdon*, 1968

Robinson, David, *Chaplin: His Life and Art*, 1985

—, *Chaplin : The Mirror of Opinion*, 1983

Sennett, Mack, with Cameron Shipp, *King of Comedy*, 1954

Sklar, Robert, *Film: An International History of the Medium*, 1993

Smith, Julian, *Chaplin*, 1986

Sobel, Raoul, and David Francis, *Chaplin: Genesis of a Clown*, 1977

LIST OF ILLUSTRATIONS

CHAPTER 3

CHAPTER 4

DOCUMENTS

INDEX

ACKNOWLEDGMENTS

The publishers thank Mme Pamela Paumier from the Chaplin archives (© Roy Export Company Establishment, Paris) as well as the Chaplin family for their help in preparing this book.

PHOTO CREDITS

All the illustrations come from the Chaplin archives (© Roy Export Company Establishment, Paris, and © Bubbles Incorporated S. A. ®), except for the following: Archive Photos France, Paris, 3, 60b, 66b, 104, 105, 107, 110–1, 111, 112. Cahiers du cinéma, Paris, 101. Cinémathèque française, Paris, 29. Peter Jackson Collection, London, 13, 18a. David Robinson, London, back cover, spine, 14r, 15a, 15b, 16–7, 18b, 20a, 20b, 22, 32r, 38b, 38–9a, 40–1, 41a, 50bl, 51r, 52a, 56r, 58b, 68r, 74l, 76a, 76b, 92b, 102, 103b, 108–9.

TEXT CREDITS

Grateful acknowledgment is made for use of material from the following works: (inside front cover, pp. 14, 19, 24–5, 25, 31, 33, 35, 55, 63, 71, 122–3, 123–4, 124, 125) Charlie Chaplin, *My Autobiography*, The Bodley Head, 1964; reprinted with permission of the Estate of Charles Chaplin and Random House UK Ltd, London. (pp. 120–1) Charlie Chaplin, 'Pantomime and Comedy', *The New York Times*, 25 January 1931; copyright © 1931 by The New York Times Company. Reprinted by permission. (pp. 128–9) Max Linder in *Le Film*, 1919, translated in David Robinson, *Chaplin: The Mirror of Opinion*, 1983; reprinted with permission of David Robinson.

David Robinson
is an internationally respected film critic
and historian. He was for many years resident critic
of *The Financial Times* and subsequently *The Times*,
to which he still contributes regularly.
His books include *Buster Keaton* (1969),
World Cinema (1973), *Chaplin: The Mirror of
Opinion* (1983), *Chaplin: His Life and Art* (1985),
Music of the Shadows (1990), *Masterpieces of
Animation: 1833–1908* (1991), *Richard Attenborough*
(1992) and *Georges Méliès* (1993), among other titles.
An authority on the pre-history of cinema,
he has organized many exhibitions
on cinema-related subjects.

© Gallimard 1995

This edition © Thames and Hudson Ltd,
London, 1996

British Library Cataloguing-in-Publication Data

A catalogue record for this book is available from
the British Library

ISBN 0–500–30063–1

Printed and bound in Italy
by Editoriale Libraria, Trieste